States of Scotland 2004

States of Scotland
2004

edited by
Kenneth Roy

ICS Books
Glasgow

First published in Great Britain in 2003 by
ICS Books
Institute of Contemporary Scotland
Suite 304B, The Pentagon Centre,
Washington Street, Glasgow G3 8AZ

ISBN 0 9546527 1 1

Typeset by Carrick Publishing Ltd
Printed in Great Britain by The Cromwell Press

All the contributors to this book worked for nothing – that is to say, no fee – on the understanding that any profits would be devoted to the humanitarian work of the Institute of Contemporary Scotland. I wish to acknowledge here their benevolence, as well as their wisdom and authority. I wish also to thank Maggie Lennon, who contributed so much to the commissioning and editing of States of Scotland 2004, as well as my colleagues at Carrick Publishing Ltd for getting the book to press on time, despite an extraordinarily tight schedule. – KR

Contents

Part IV
Where We Live

Part V
Culture of Scotland

Preface

It is now four years since the "devolution settlement" produced the first directly-elected Scottish Parliament. How is the new Scotland faring – not only politically, but economically and culturally? The signs and portents are often confusing if not contradictory. This book is an attempt to make some sense of them.

States of Scotland is not, strictly speaking, a review of the year; when the articles were written, 2003 was not quite over. Nor is it in any sense an official report or survey. Rather it is a collection of intensely personal perspectives, written by authorities on the many subjects under review. The twenty-one essays on matters ranging from film to football, politics to poetry, law to literature, economics to education add up to a formidable body of expertise and insight. Although I make no claims for comprehensivity – science and music being notable omissions – the scope is as wide as could reasonably be expected in a single volume.

There were no rules governing editorial tone or content: our contributors had a precious freedom to write at length and in depth in any style that suited them. The approach varies from the passionately involved (John McAllion on his disappointed expectations of the Parliament, Norma Bennie on public attitudes to mental illness) to the more dispassionately inquiring and sceptical (Walter Humes on education). Many of the essayists took a view of modern Scotland that this editor found surprisingly positive (Gavin Reid on the Scottish economy, Tom Hubbard on literature, Robert Black on justice, among others). The pessimists are relatively few. A common theme is that many good things have happened in Scotland which would not have happened, or not happened so quickly, had it not been for devolution. And the book is not short on practical ideas for further improvement, including an imaginative proposal for dealing with the Scottish curse of sectarianism.

The book opens with the view (in Kay Carmichael's introductory essay) that our small society consists of many diverse communities; and ends with Angus Peter Campbell's vision that, in one small community, all aspects of that society are reflected, for better or ill. Between these extremes, there is a great deal of Scotland.

I hope that *States of Scotland* will become an annual publication holding a mirror to the contemporary scene. The only surprise is that, so much having changed in Scotland and with so much more about to change, such a publication did not exist before.

Kenneth Roy
Glasgow
November 2003

Contributors

Rowena Arshad, OBE
Race
Director of the Centre for Education for Racial Equality in Scotland (CERES) and a lecturer in equity and rights. Equal Opportunities Commissioner for Scotland, having been the Commission's first-ever black woman member. Member of the STUC General Council.

Norma Bennie
Mental Health
A healthcare manager with Renfrewshire and Inverclyde Primary Care Trust and a former Vice-Chair of the Mental Welfare Commission for Scotland, with whom she was a commissioner for six years.

Professor Robert Black, QC
Law
Professor of Scots Law at the University of Edinburgh and a world-renowned expert on the Lockerbie disaster. Former temporary Sheriff.

Angus Peter Campbell
The Gaels
Poet, novelist and journalist. Born on South Uist and now lives on Skye, where he is the Iain Crichton Smith Writing Fellow for Highland Council.

Kay Carmichael
Society
Former psychiatric social worker and senior lecturer at Glasgow University. Helped to create the Scottish children's panels, was Deputy Chairperson of the Supplementary Benefits Commission and a member of Harold Wilson's policy unit at 10 Downing Street.

Roger Crofts, CBE
The Natural Environment
Lecturer, writer and advisor on environmental and rural affairs issues. Former Chief Executive of Scottish Natural Heritage.

Duncan Davidson
Medicine
Former Consultant Neurologist with Tayside Health Board and former Honorary Senior Lecturer in Medicine at the University of Dundee. Now working on the IVIMEDS programme into virtual medicine being pioneered by the University of Dundee.

Jim Delahunt
Sport
Sports presenter for Scottish Television's *Scotsport* and *Monday Night Live* and a sports columnist with the *Sunday Herald*. Former amateur footballer and jockey.

John Gerrard
The Built Environment
After working in local government in England, came to Scotland in 1968 as Assistant Director of the Scottish Civic Trust, with whom he worked for the next thirty-one years.

Tom Hubbard
Literature
Editor of the Bibliography of Scottish Literature in translation (BOSLIT) at Edinburgh University and the National Library of Scotland. First librarian, Scottish Poetry Library.

Walter Humes

Education

Professor of Education at the University of Strathclyde and former Head of Educational Studies at the University of Glasgow. A former Editor of the *Scottish Educational Review.*

John Izod

Film

Professor of Screen Analysis at the University of Stirling and former Dean of the Faculty of Arts. A former Governor of the Scottish Film Council.

R D Kernohan, OBE

Religion

Writer, journalist and broadcaster who started his journalistic career with the *Glasgow Herald.* Former Editor of *Life and Work* and former Director-General of Scottish Conservative Central Office.

Magnus Linklater

Broadcasting

Writer, journalist and broadcaster, a columnist with the *Times* and *Scotland on Sunday* and former Editor of the *Scotsman.* Former Chairman of the Scottish Arts Council and of the Edinburgh Book Festival.

Gail MacDonald

Theatre

A Fellow of The Young Scotland Programme and former Marketing Manager of Grey Coast Theatre Company in Wick. Following Grey Coast's loss of grant funding, she was made redundant and now works for Scotsman Publications Ltd.

John McAllion

Politics and Parliament

Former Labour MP and MSP for Dundee East. Before entering Parliament, he was Convenor of Tayside Regional Council and a member of the Scottish Executive of the Labour Party. Currently a campaigner with Oxfam in Scotland.

Cordelia Oliver
Art
Former art critic of the *Glasgow Herald* and the *Guardian.*

Tessa Ransford, OBE
Poetry
Poet. Founder and former Director of the Scottish Poetry Library. Writing Fellow at the Centre for Human Ecology and former Editor of *Lines Review*. Recently appointed Chairman of Scottish PEN International.

Gavin Reid
Business and Economics
Professor of Economics at St Andrews University and Director of the Centre for Research into Industry, Enterprise, Finance and the Firm (CRIEFF). He has taught both in the UK and abroad and is Past President of the Scottish Economic Society.

Harry Reid
Journalism
Journalist and writer, who worked in the Scottish press for thirty-two years. A former Editor of the *Herald*. In 2001 he received honorary doctorates from Edinburgh and Glasgow Universities for his services to Scottish journalism.

Kenneth Roy
Editor, States of Scotland
Founder-Director of the Institute of Contemporary Scotland and of the Young Scotland Programme, and founder Editor of the *Scottish Review*. Former daily columnist on the *Scotsman* and former weekly columnist on the *Observer*. Former Columnist of the Year in the *UK Press Gazette* national press awards and twice Scottish Critic of the Year.

Fred Shedden

Sectarianism

A retired solicitor and company director and Chair of the anti-sectarian charity, Nil By Mouth. He is a member of the Scottish Further Education Funding Council and serves on the management committee of the Glasgow Housing Association.

Introductory essay

Society

Kay Carmichael

Born in Glasgow and having lived there all my life, I think of myself as a Glaswegian. If however, when outside Scotland, I'm asked where I come from I have no hesitation in saying Scotland. This is not because I think my home town may not be recognised. It is rather because a sense of identity with Scotland takes over in the face of the outside world, the "others", beyond our borders. The part of me which claims that identity of being Scottish, is sometimes surprised. I know I am different from Edinburgh folk, some would say Edinburgh is a different country. I know I am different from those who live in the Western Isles or the Borders. I am irretrievably a Glaswegian, yet in the face of what I might almost call the enemy, I am a Scot and as such a member of a Scottish society – whatever that word might mean.

Few of us think of ourselves as living in a society. If forced to identify ourselves we would probably admit to being a member of a community – perhaps even several communities. What, if any, is the difference? The academics suggest that in Europe it was the Renaissance that marked the transition from "community" to "society", when an appreciation of a wider world than previously known was developed. What we have now in Scotland, and it may be the same everywhere, is a collection of communities within a wider structure which we define as our society. Looking at what is different between the two, it seems that indigenous communities, which are made up of groups of people living together, have held on to a relatively unchanged way of life. In these the basis of human relationships was and is primarily emotional. The individuals who make up the community are linked in some way. It can be bonds of blood, of faith, mystic ties with the land where they live or by shared traditions, jokes or accent.

There are other communities which are not indigenous but are created for some particular purpose – to meet some need within the wider society. These are cultural or instrumental in their function. Some may grow out of musical, literary or artistic aspirations which can be met in extra-mural activities or we see the passionate creation of the Scottish Socialist Party which gives a home to a community of people with aspirations to change the nature of the society in which they live. More prosaic but equally essential communities are to be found in the institutions which represent shared interests — for our trade unionists from the Fire Brigades Union to the EIS or the National Union of Teachers, for religious people a range of churches, for voluntary workers a range of good causes.

The indigenous communities in our country come together with a group of neighbouring communities, under a common umbrella to be able to deal more effectively with local problems. But the shift to a Scottish society comes about as a consequence of the totality of indigenous communities choosing to live within a common structure. In this way they are strengthened by a central government which can focus on and legislate for issues which may be too difficult, controversial or sensitive for the small community – issues like racism, sexism or the minimum wage. But this development forces a public emphasis primarily on the rationality of human social and political organisations. What is sometimes not recognised is that while respecting their rationality, there is a need to build into the central structure an understanding of the traditional and emotional intelligence of the smaller units of community.

Rational thought and discussion as distinct from a traditional and emotional response is an essential basis for a democratic society so we enter a new dimension of communication. A community has much less pressure to be democratic, regulated, as so often it is, by internal emotional factors rather than by external rational arrangements. The community may be no less effective for that. Decisions will usually be reached by a sophisticated network of informal communication between the people involved. So we have these two forces functioning at the same time. The kind of society in which we live in Scotland, and any changes which have taken place within it, have arisen as a result of the interaction between them. Our wider society's capacity to move forward in interesting and challenging ways is very dependent on a creative rather than a destructive relationship with the communities which have retained coherence within it. The notion of moving forward – of change, what is changing and how we can influence that change – is one with which I am primarily concerned.

Scotland, having so recently achieved a degree of autonomy over its affairs as a result of the new Parliament, has a particular need to address this issue. Flexibility is a key characteristic of a modern democratic society. The flow of ideas and decisions should be as little as possible hampered by unhelpful pre-established norms or patterns, while helpful strengths should be identified and retained. Our society has tasks to consider which are relevant to the here and now of our lives and the lives of our fellow citizens. We can see ourselves as having turned over a new page on which are written new questions to which we must begin to find answers while recognising that those answers will in turn lead to new questions. As Eugene Ionesco said, "It is not the answer that enlightens but the question." But how do we find what questions to ask among the plethora of issues that we see and hear every day in the press, on radio and television? In responding to this hubbub each of us looks through a personal lens which focuses on some subjects and sees those clearly, distorts others in ways that suit our prejudices and blots others out altogether. What is common to every lens is a sense of morality. Is what I am seeing good or bad?

Currently we seem constantly to see and hear examples of the bad. The notion that our society is collapsing as a result of dishonesty, anti-authoritarianism, drug-taking, criminal behaviour and sexual corruption is constantly thrust before us. It is not surprising if the lens with which we view our world becomes clouded and the questions we might ask influenced by depression and lack of confidence. Every chapter in this book is focused through a particular lens, with writers who are hoping to be consciously aware of the pitfalls. I am offering you my lens for what I see as good or bad on a few questions which I believe may illuminate the current situation and suggest some priorities for the future shaping of our society.

To return to the issue of a corrupt, collapsing society. We have to acknowledge that all is not well. I dislike the way young people eat and drink walking along the street and throw down paper and cans on the pavement. But it might help if there were more rubbish bins. I dislike the graffiti on walls but often admire the skill and imagination they show. I would like to see large boards made available for the use of these young people who, if born into a different social class, might be using their talents in taking a degree in art or design. To change behaviour we dislike we have either to remove the causes or else offer more constructive outlets. There are always reasons for the behaviour we deplore but we have to seek them out.

I've used the word "class" in the previous paragraph. We still have in Scotland clear, destructive social class distinctions and that is something I would like to see changed. Inequality is deeply embedded in our society and many of the behaviours of which people complain grow out of that inequality. We all come into this world with potential. But our expectations of health, education, housing, work and creativity are decided, not only by that potential, but to a great extent by the social situation of the family and the community into which we are born. In Scotland it appears that roughly a quarter of our children are exposed from birth to living in an environment filled with the stresses inevitably associated with poverty – poor housing, inadequate food, parental anxiety about bills, in due course overcrowded, under-staffed schools and the assumption that there is no good future for them to look forward to. They are also exposed to the high incidence in their community of murder, suicide, alcoholism, drug taking and mental illness. When these experiences occur, as they also do, in a prosperous environment, while they may cause distress, money offers privacy from public curiosity and space within the family home which makes retreat and time for healing possible.

What opportunities do these disadvantaged children have to identify with the wider society? They will in fact feel alienated from it. We know that delinquency and various other forms of anti-social behaviour, which the political guardians of society are so anxious to clamp down on, come most strongly to the fore as the school leaving age approaches. That is precisely the point where the realities of inequality are at their sharpest, namely at the point of entry into the labour market. There are sharp discrepancies between any expectations they may have managed to retain and the opportunities available to them. What is even more distressing is that it appears that at this stage they become aware of the fact that this situation is not likely to improve.

All this takes place in the realisation that the wider society as represented by teachers and bureaucrats at every level of encounter sees them as failures. This is particularly acute for the young males in the community who may well attempt to find areas of status for themselves in fighting with their peers or in sexually dominating the young women they encounter. That domination may well result in an unplanned pregnancy since the buying and use of condoms involves a degree of planning at odds with the sense of meaninglessness of any other form of planning. The lens through which they see the world will most likely, and not surprisingly, be coated with anger. Again we may see this sense of failure among some boys from fee-paying schools who also react in macho style but the consequences for them are rather different. They are neither written off, since some kind of job will be found for them, nor are they liable to be picked up by the police for fighting.

At this stage more fortunate children are confidently planning which specialist subjects to take to go on to higher education or if leaving school expect to have a good chance of getting a socially acceptable job. These are not the youngsters who are going to be rounded up by the police for hanging around street corners. Nor are they so likely to have been exposed to the seedier experiences of life. Their health is likely to be better and they are more likely to have an image, if only a vague one, of their future lives. They will expect at some stage to have a sexual partner and a home. If the relationship is heterosexual they will expect to have children and when they do will see these children as an investment in the future for which, if they haven't done it before, they will now begin to plan. What is remarkable is how many young people in our deprived communities survive their early environment to create stable lives and families. The key to this for both young men and young women is if they can get a job. This will determine the pattern of the rest of their lives and the lives of their children.

What is striking about our society is that an hour in the out-patient department of any hospital enables you to identify the social class of all the patients. It is as obvious as that. I know of no other European country where that is the case. We do live in Europe, we do not live in the Third World. We live in a rich country where high levels of income make gross levels of spending on homes, clothing, cars, holidays and everyday expenditure possible for a significant proportion of those whom we call fellow citizens. Bottles of wine, each costing several hundreds of pounds, are available in our posh restaurants. Both men and women in the upper income levels will pay hundreds, even thousands, of pounds for a coat or a suit. It is impossible to ignore the injustice of our acute poverty side by side with these displays of wealth. Yet when people talk as I described earlier of a corrupt, collapsing society, this is not one of the issues they raise. I suggest we have to ask ourselves if we are happy to live in such a society and if not what can we do to change it? How do we want to live together?

Before turning to that, perhaps another question to ask is — what is our current sense of identity as members of our society? Is it open to change, is it in the process of change and if so what is shaping our sense of identity at the moment? I believe it is changing and changing for the better. We are more tolerant in religious matters, we have a more international vision, we have more respect for our culture and our language than we had in the past. One development that may seem insignificant but is really quite fundamental, can be seen in the move to demilitarise bagpipe music. Musicians are rewriting it to change its style but to retain it as being distinctively Scottish rather than engaged in British militarism. It also appears that we are more welcoming to visitors. The majority of Glaswegians have welcomed asylum seekers and across the city, centres run by church volunteers and local authority staff are helping provide basic essentials for these families who have nothing. These are signs of confidence that we can take strangers into our country without our sense of identity being threatened. The significant Scottish contribution to the anti-war debate has a place in this roll call of actions. It is worth noting that all these indications of strength have come not from the state, not from the churches or the major political parties, but from the grass roots.

We have to remember that as Scots we live in a society within a society. Not all the decisions taken about that society are within our jurisdiction nor the ones we may want to take. We have that limitation on a sense of being able, as a nation, to run our own affairs. The importance of a Scottish Parliament should not be underestimated but it appears that in some quarters the move towards a politically independent Scotland is growing rather than diminishing. This sense of being able to make changes is important because it is the basis for hope in personal as well as political life. In order to have change we have to have hope; in order to have hope we must have the sense that change is possible.

I have spent some time on the question of our unequal society but we could say – why should we worry about an unequal society? If we're doing all right ourselves, why bother? I won't go in here to a theoretical discussion of the case for social justice. I will assume that you, my reader, are well informed on those arguments. Let me approach you on the simple basis of self interest. It will also meet the demands of social justice so we have a double bonus. We know that within national societies rich people are healthier and live longer than poor people; but when comparisons are made between societies it is not the richest but – roughly speaking — the more equal societies that live longest. In unequal societies reduced life expectancy affects up to sixty percent of the population – that is to say even the middle income groups. More equal societies find it easier to create good health and social security services – partly because they cost less than they would in unequal societies, partly because they have produced more nurses and doctors. There are complex reasons for these facts outwith the scope of this chapter. I have to ask you to take them on trust. More equal societies find also that their people are more willing to vote and pay taxes for these services – because everybody uses them, and they do not feel so distanced socially from the poor patient in the next bed or in the waiting room. Better services make the nation both more equal and healthier.

Perhaps more striking is the fact that inequality is a source of social instability. Much of this instability grows out of the alienation of young people. I am not concerned only with the social implications of this instability. The financial implications alone are highly significant. I am deeply concerned with the human cost in pain experienced by the young people and their families. Being taken into care, being shut up in a young offenders' institution or in a prison is not an experience conducive to creating a positive attitude to life. We have to understand that the vast majority of the anti-social behaviour which disrupts our social processes from the nursery school up is directly related to issues of inequality. We have to understand that it is within our ability to change that. A society which contains, as ours does, large numbers of people who experience social and economic deprivation is characterised by resignation and acceptance at every level. That is not something we can tolerate.

How can we move to a society which is healthier in every sense of that word – a society in which we can all look each other in the face with both respect and self-respect? First we have to recognise that the way we live now does not make that possible. Second we have to be convinced that change is possible. It means accepting the need for some redistribution of wealth. That is not an impossible thought in a society that has found the money to fight five wars in six years. How should we use the money?

My personal preference would be to start with the provision of support services to families with infants who are living in poverty. Indeed the support should start during the pregnancy and continue through until nursery school provision becomes appropriate. All primary schools and secondary schools should be so staffed as to make small classes possible. This more than anything else would make classroom disruption unlikely since it would make better relationships between teachers and pupils possible.

A classroom should be seen as a small community linked by

democratic relationships. Anyone wanting to leave at fifteen or sixteen should have access to some form of skills training good enough to be held in as much esteem as a university degree. Throughout their school lives children should have easy and non-judgmental access to group and individual counselling services which enable them to discuss personal and family issues. Primary in this should be small group discussion of sexuality, both heterosexual and homosexual, contraception and abortion and some thoughtful understanding of the feelings and needs of the opposite sex.

These are my thoughts about our society as it is now. I write them knowing that they need to be shared and discussed before they can be acted on. Other people may have different priorities for action from mine. But first we all need to be convinced that action is morally and socially necessary. What I believe we should be doing is reclaiming the traditions of our smaller, indigenous communities in which everyone was seen as having a place, no matter what contribution they were able to make. To translate this to the wider society, to make it a more equal and fairer place, would be a mind-blowing achievement, one which would light a beacon for the countries with whom we share this island, and one I believe to be possible.

I believe this because in Scotland we also have much to celebrate. We have strengths reflected in our literature and our poetry. You will read of these joyful aspects of our lives in other pages of this book. We are past the stage now in Scotland where we simply want to survive. We are ready now to be a creative force, creating a society in which we can look at each other and at the stranger with self-respect and confidence.

Part I

Estates of Scotland

Politics and Parliament
Education
Business and Economics
Law
Religion
Medicine

Part I: Estates of Scotland

Politics and Parliament

John McAllion

Sixteen years ago, in the immediate aftermath of Margaret Thatcher's third election victory, William McIlvanney delivered a speech to the SNP conference in Dundee on the theme of "Stands Scotland Where It Did?" The speech took as its starting point an exchange between two characters in a scene from *Macbeth*. In answer to the question, comes the reply: "Alas, poor country. Almost afraid to know itself."

McIlvanney builds on this exchange to deliver a lecture dripping in contempt for the Thatcherite values being forced onto the Scotland of the 1980s. He warns the SNP conference that, unless Scotland rejects these values along with Thatcher's government, then it may lose altogether its historic sense of itself as a nation serious about the search for social justice.

He cautions that were we to accept what Thatcher was doing to our country, then it would lead to catastrophe and to us wakening not too many years from now "...to find that we no longer live where we thought we lived." The real Scotland that he believed had developed from the experience and the pain and the long thought and deep humanity of the Scottish people would be "gone". The Scotland we would then inhabit would be "...a desert of dependency – a land of lost principles, of decayed traditions, of ruined ideals."

McIlvanney was not to know that 1987 would be Thatcher's last personal electoral triumph. He could not foresee that within a decade there would be a Labour landslide majority in Westminster and, two years after that, the establishment of Scotland's first ever democratically elected Parliament. Nor could he have imagined that, another two years on from then, we would see a second historic Labour landslide that would reduce the once dominant Tories to a splintered right-wing rump, rent by internal party strife, and irrelevant to the future government of Scotland or the United Kingdom.

So can Mclvanney's doom-laden warnings from the late 1980s now be dismissed as the exaggerations of a writer too sensitive by far and out of touch with political reality? Certainly, there are many in the political elite of Scotland today who would argue precisely that, or they would if they ever took the trouble to read his speech or to give it even a second's serious consideration. Scotland's New Labour elite would certainly claim that their period of incumbency since 1997 has represented a decisive break with the Tory hegemony of the 1980s and a return to the enduring common values and common beliefs of that other Scotland that McIlvanney feared for.

In fact, another speech delivered in the immediate aftermath of the 2003 Scottish election echoed McIlvanney's 1987 speech. On this occasion it was one given to the Scottish conference of the centre-left think tank Progress by that rising New Labour star and rather spooky MP, Douglas Alexander. In it he asks his rather different audience "Stands Scotland Where it Did?" Sixteen years on, he gives a very different answer.

Alexander was speaking just seven weeks after Scottish New Labour had recorded the lowest Labour vote in a national election since 1931. It was no accident, then, that even this most "New" of Scottish Labour MPs referred throughout the speech to "Labour" rather than "New Labour". Those who seek to sell political allegiance and commitment as just another consumer brand in the market place recognise better than most when the new brand is not working.

To be fair to Alexander, he has a reputation as a New Labour thinker and had obviously read the McIlvanney speech. In his own speech he argued that it was Labour values that continued to define Scotland's future. Yet when you search for the meaning of these Labour values in the text of his speech, there is little there of any substance. The speech is almost exclusively an exercise in beating

Labour's electoral drum. He boasts that successive electoral victories have redrawn the political map, halted the swinging of the electoral pendulum, smashed Labour's main enemies and secured it sustained incumbency both at Westminster and Holyrood. Not so much triumphalist as millenarian!

If he defined these Labour values as having any political substance at all, then it was in terms of the Scottish people being anti-independence and pro-devolution within continuing British authority. He also presented Labour as being less extreme than the Tories on free markets. This is poor fare from a party apologist who claims that today's Labour Party stands in the same tradition as Keir Hardie, Clause 4 and the Red Clydesiders. The Liberal Party that Hardie deserted to form Labour had a more radical appeal. Maxton's Independent Labour Party would never have dreamed of affiliating to a party as pro-market or centrist as Alexander's.

New Labour apologists, of course, would argue that such thinking is outdated and irrelevant to these times, when the power of global markets demands a different political response. They would point to a list of their achievements as evidence that they are the only serious political force capable of delivering traditional values in the modern setting of globalisation. Most of us are by now familiar with these litanies of self-congratulation, usually beginning with the independence of the Bank of England and ending with the lowest interest rates in thirty years.

Nor would most of us dispute that there have been substantial achievements and, chief among them, a Scottish Parliament elected by proportional representation. This had been a dream on the Scottish Left for generations. If that were New Labour's only achievement, we all would remain in its debt. Yet there are grounds for questioning whether this is a New Labour achievement at all.

The commitment to the Scottish Parliament was inherited by New Labour. It was never its creation. Those who deserve credit for the final success are the earlier generations of political activists, inside and outside of the labour movement, who struggled for a century and more to see it brought into existence. New Labour came into office in 1997 with no alternative other than to deliver a Scottish Parliament.

Scottish New Labour's unique contribution to date has been to ensure that the new Parliament keeps to its limited and subsidiary role under the "sovereign" Parliament in the Palace of Westminster. It is no accident that Jack McConnell sees the role of the Parliament as doing less but doing it better. Nor is it surprising that New Labour's vision for our first-ever democratic Parliament is that it should concentrate on issues that until now have been the remit of local government. Let MSPs deal with anti-social behaviour, fly tipping and fireworks. The real matters of state are for our political superiors in Westminster, who will set the limits of our competence and authority.

Indeed most of the achievements that New Labour claims for itself are either open to question or are subject to heavy qualification. The record investment in Scotland's schools and hospitals is spoiled by the fact that most of it comes in the form of run-for-profit hospital and school buildings and a massive sell-off of hospital estates at rock bottom prices to the private sector. The new Edinburgh Royal Infirmary has beside every bed a console that includes a combined radio/TV/computer/telephone. Access to this hi-tech console is available on a rising scale of charges paid to the private company with the contract for all new PFI hospitals. If you can't afford the charges, you only get one hour's free TV in the morning and all day free radio. Hi-tech consoles are not for the poor.

Even the additional help to Scotland's pensioners comes wrapped in the hated means test. The national minimum wage is set below the poverty line. Housing stock transfer is driven not by tenant empowerment but by the enrichment of private investors. The deserving or working poor are given tax credits to boost their poverty wages. The undeserving or unemployed poor are bullied and harassed into the worst of work situations. Few notice that the real beneficiaries of Irn Broon's largesse are the skinflint employers who refuse to pay their workers a living wage.

A warm Scottish welcome is given to rich economic migrants who can bring with them the resources and the skills desperately needed in Scotland, while poor asylum seekers fleeing persecution and terror are denied rights and sometimes locked up. It's still money and wealth we throw open our doors to, not people. The list of examples could go on and on. How can the party formed by the unions refuse to repeal anti-union laws, among the most restrictive in Europe, imposed by the Tories?

The trouble with New Labour is that it tries to be two different things at the same time. It wants to be seen as standing in the social democratic traditions of earlier Labour governments. It wants to help the poor, to redistribute wealth in their favour, to deliver quality public services. However, it wants even more to be the party of business, to support corporate power, deregulated markets and economic efficiency. It cannot grasp that these two different poles of desire cannot be reconciled. New Labour cannot be the party of capital and of labour at the same time. It therefore ends up as a strange hybrid, a political mutation never before seen in our times – a neo-liberal wolf in social democratic sheep's clothing.

Is such a political beast the first sighting of that other Scotland McIlvanney warned against sixteen years ago? It might be if New Labour was all there was to Scottish politics. Thankfully, it is not. McIlvanney spoke at the conference of the SNP back then. He thanked them then for reminding not only ourselves but Westminster of who we were over a very long period of time. He rightly recognised the absolutely central role of the SNP in forcing the national question on to the centre stage of Scottish politics in the post-war era. So, stands the SNP where it did?

"Alas, poor party. Almost afraid to know itself." To paraphrase Harold Wilson, the SNP is a national crusade or it is nothing. The near breakthrough in 1974, when eleven nationalist MPs were elected on a third of the vote across Scotland, came out of nowhere and shook the Scottish Labour establishment to its foundations. It represented an emotional outburst from a country beginning to lose out in the balance of UK power and determined not to be left to fester. Scottish Labour's commitment to home rule was thereafter driven more by fear of the SNP than anything else.

Without the SNP, the Wilson and Callaghan governments would never have introduced their flawed proposals for a Scottish Assembly. But for the electoral threat their party posed, there may never have been a Scottish Constitutional Convention to open the way for the Lib-Lab consensus that finally delivered Donald Dewar's white paper. The SNP campaigned as positively as any party for a yes/yes vote in the referendum. They played their part in bringing about the Parliament on the Mound and deserve great credit for it.

Although he himself was never a member of the SNP, it is clear from his remarks in 1987 that McIlvanney genuinely respected the role played by the SNP in Scottish politics. It is far from clear that he would continue to do so today. Somewhere between then and now the SNP changed.

They lost their best-known and most able leader when Alex Salmond all but retired back down to London. They split with charismatic personalities such as Jim Sillars and Margo MacDonald. They forced the colourful campaigner, Dorothy Grace Elder, to leave the party. They succeeded in losing their most able parliamentarians in Mike Russell and Andrew Wilson. They scared off rising young talents like Duncan Hamilton. The elections of 1999 might have marked the high water mark of SNP electoral success with thirty-five seats. By the time of the 2003 elections it was clear that they had no idea how to handle such success.

More depressingly, they were showing every sign of taking New Labour as their model for electoral success. Flush with the funding for research and offices that comes with electoral success, the SNP became yet another professional political party. Their offices were suddenly awash with thrusting young professionals armed with focus group findings and arguments for driving the party on to the centre ground where all modern elections are allegedly fought and won. The old guard of fundamentalists was pushed to the side as the new on-message politicos took over. They even managed to start an internal row over whether they were really committed to independence for Scotland.

They claimed to be newer than New Labour. They, not New Labour, were the party of Scottish business. By slashing Scottish taxes they would release the potential of Scotland's entrepreneurs. They would ensure that Scotland's dynamic market economy was fully integrated into the global economy. They would be tougher on crime, have more Scottish bobbies on the beat, crack down on social disorder. They had become in effect New Labour with a kilt on. Even Maggie would have approved their new political clothes.

They too had thrown over the idealism that had driven their earlier success and so frightened the unionist establishment. This new SNP was far easier for that establishment to deal with. The party split over their new political direction. An almost unknown party activist from Glasgow who had never held any elected office took almost a fifth of the party vote in a challenge to John Swinney's leadership. Swinney himself failed to win the support of around a third of party members in that vote. Four years into the lifetime of the Scottish Parliament, the SNP remained divided, demoralised and defeated for the umpteenth time in general elections.

As for the Tories, they claimed a moral victory in winning three out of seventy-two first past the post seats and fifteen list seats on a fifteen per cent share of the second vote. This Tory "revival" had begun two years earlier when they had managed to win one Scottish seat in the UK general election. Their leader David McLetchie could sound upbeat about these appalling results only because the Tory wipe-out in 1997 had been so disastrous that things really could only get better for the Tories thereafter. Nevertheless, as the only political party ever to take more than fifty per cent of the vote in a Scottish election (1955), the Scottish Tories had now ceased to be a truly national political force. They had been reduced to a political rump. Other parties were now sitting firmly on the political ground they had once held alone.

The Lib Dems, of course, were now firmly inside the New Labour fold as coalition partners. They huffed and puffed about pulling New Labour to the left of centre ground on issues such as tuition fees and free personal care for the elderly. While there is an element of truth in such claims, New Labour was never pulled anywhere it really didn't want to go. If anything, New Labour was pulling the Lib Dems where they did not want to go, as is evident from the locking up of child asylum seekers and the electronic tagging of under-sixteens. The lust for office often involves the losing of long-cherished principles. The Lib Dems were learning that harsh reality all over again after almost a century of principled opposition.

Between them, these four parties took ninety per cent of the first vote and seventy-eight per cent of the second vote in the most recent Scottish general election. They are what Scottish politics have become in the new millennium. Parties clustered together on the centre ground. Parties committed to market capitalism and to business. Parties of law and order. Parties of low taxation and limits on public spending and borrowing. Parties who will be tough on immigration. McIlvanney must look at them and wonder if we really have now arrived at that Scotland of "lost principles", "decayed traditions" and "ruined ideals".

In a recent review of the latest biography of Margaret Thatcher, Lord Hurd mentioned that she had regarded her greatest achievement as the creation of New Labour. She obviously believed that she had so altered the dynamic of British politics in her time that no party could thereafter come to power other than by embracing her free market principles and instinct for social and economic order. She claims to have achieved what she had set out to achieve – the destruction of British socialism. From here on in, we are all capitalists now.

Looking at the four main Scottish political parties, it is difficult to argue against such a thesis. They are all cut from the same cloth as New Labour. They all conform to Thatcher's stereotype capitalist party. They all must be a huge disappointment to McIlvanney and to his aspiration for Scotland as a nation serious about the search for social justice. There is no social justice to be found in the embrace of global capitalism.

Yet, these parties do not represent the whole of Scottish politics. The Greens, the SSP and the independents made important breakthroughs in this same election. Socialism, environmentalism and radicalism survived, albeit in very different forms from those we had become accustomed to. Most importantly, the majority of voters were so turned off that they failed to vote at all. That other Scotland has not "gone", as McIlvanney feared. It still survives. It merely needs to be re-awakened, re-energised. That is the political task for the new millennium. There is still hope. There is always hope.

Part I: Estates of Scotland

Education

Walter Humes

The political context

Since the re-establishment of the Scottish Parliament in 1999 there have been no less than four ministers in charge of the Scottish Executive Education Department (SEED) – first Sam Galbraith, followed by Jack McConnell, Cathy Jamieson and the present incumbent Peter Peacock. This rapid turnover raises important questions about continuity and leadership in educational policy. The nature of modern political life is such that each minister is under pressure to make his or her mark as quickly as possible, so stamping personal authority on the ministerial portfolio. Usually this takes the form of launching a series of "consultation" exercises (the results of which can often be predicted in advance) and "initiatives" (complete with smiling children, photo opportunities and overblown press releases). Another favoured strategy is the setting up of "task groups" charged with coming up with simple solutions to intractable problems (such as truancy and indiscipline in schools). Before these various approaches can be properly evaluated, the minister who introduced them has either moved on to higher office (as in the case of the First Minister, Jack McConnell) or passed into political obscurity (the fate of Sam Galbraith).

On any rational analysis, this is no way to run any organisation, far less an important public service such as education. Defenders of the system might say that a great deal of the day-to-day business of education is carried out by administrators and professionals who generally enjoy greater continuity and security of tenure than politicians and who are more committed to a long-term view. But who are these administrators and professionals and how accountable are they in the democratic process?

At national level there are senior civil servants such as Mike Ewart, Head of SEED, and Edward Frizzell, Head of the Enterprise and Lifelong Learning Department which deals with further and higher education. These are important figures but generally not well known even among teachers and other education "insiders". This is also true of Graham Donaldson who is in charge of Her Majesty's Inspectorate of Education (HMIE). Then there are the heads of non-governmental bodies such as the Scottish Qualifications Authority (SQA), Learning and Teaching Scotland (LTS) and the General Teaching Council (GTC). Taken together, these people constitute the upper levels of the policy community in Scottish education with strong links to each other and ready access to government. How adequate is their stewardship, bearing in mind the strong claims that have traditionally been made about the quality of Scottish education compared to other countries?

In the 2002 Reith Lectures Baroness Onora O'Neill identified a crisis of trust in public life, whereby the traditional respect accorded to those holding high political and professional office is no longer forthcoming. This is certainly true of Scottish education and can easily be illustrated. In 2000 the Scottish Qualifications Authority failed to deliver accurate and timely examination results to a significant minority of students. This caused a political crisis which led to the resignation of the chief executive, the reconstitution of the SQA board, a redefined role for the inspectorate, and the replacement of the minister in charge of SEED. Since then SQA has continued to attract critical attention and in 2003 the new chief executive, who had been in post for only eighteen months, decided to quit. Public confidence in those who occupy positions of leadership is inevitably damaged by such episodes.

A less dramatic example of the decline in trust derives from the settlement following the McCrone report, *A Teaching Profession for the 21st Century* (2001). This sought to address teacher dissatisfaction by offering improved salaries and conditions of service, a better deal for newly qualified teachers, and increased opportunities for continuing professional development (through the Chartered Teacher scheme). While parts of this package have been welcomed by the majority of teachers, other aspects have caused disquiet – notably the flattening of the promotion structure for secondary teachers and the results of the so-called "job sizing" exercise, which attempted to match salary with levels of responsibility. The way in which this was carried out (by private consultants) has been widely criticised and, although current post holders will have their present salaries conserved, future holders of some posts will receive less. Again, the result has been a fair measure of disenchantment, this time within the teaching force itself. The quality of pupils' learning experiences will inevitably be influenced by the morale of teachers and so such a reaction is a cause of concern.

The official response to these points would take a variety of forms. There would be some acknowledgement that perhaps in the past a degree of complacency has been evident in establishment accounts of Scottish education. At the same time it would be pointed out that education is high on the agenda of the Scottish Parliament, that considerable resources, public and private, have been allocated to it (for example, for the building of new schools) and that there are bound to be points of tension as necessary transitions are made. It would also be pointed out that, post-devolution, there are stronger mechanisms, in the shape of parliamentary committees, whereby ministers and officials can be called to account. This is undoubtedly true, though the potential of these committees really to make a difference has not yet been fully realised. It is not entirely surprising that this should be so, since those groups used to exercising power are unlikely to give it up lightly, even if their track record in terms of achievement is patchy. In this sense what is happening in Scottish education is right at the heart of big questions to do with the evolving nature of democracy. To pursue this would involve going beyond the scope of the present chapter but it is a vital issue if the aspiration to promote greater civic activism among the Scottish people, especially the young, is to become a reality.

The official policy agenda

The Scottish Parliament approved a set of national priorities for education in 2000 and these continue to provide the framework within which schools and local authorities are expected to plan provision. The national priorities cover five areas:

Achievement and attainment
Framework for learning
Inclusion and equality
Values and citizenship
Learning for life

Like motherhood and apple pie, these general headings can readily gain a wide measure of agreement. It is when they are translated into specific aims and action points that the contested nature of educational policy becomes apparent. Following the National Debate on Scottish Education, which was conducted during Cathy Jamieson's term of office, a document entitled *Educating for Excellence* was published in 2003, which sought to give a sharper focus to the key priorities. An examination of a few of the recommendations will illustrate the difficulty of reaching an easy consensus.

One aim is to "increase pupil choice." The idea behind this is that the curriculum has become overcrowded and the scope for interesting creative work, giving pupils more scope to pursue the topics that interest them, should be increased. However, as soon as any attempt is made to reduce the compulsory core of subjects, fears about undermining the traditional breadth of Scottish education are heard. The self-interest of subject specialists, who wish to protect their own area of expertise, if necessary at the expense of others, also enters the debate about what should be compulsory and what optional.

Another aim, which is likely to gain a greater degree of support, is to "simplify and reduce the amount of assessment". The work of the upper secondary school, in particular, has been distorted by the amount of internal and external assessment that the new Higher Still courses require. Furthermore, the sheer complexity of the system, involving five levels (Access, Intermediate 1, Intermediate

2, Higher, Advanced Higher) means that even experienced teachers have difficulty understanding all the requirements. How much harder must it be for pupils, parents and employers? Once again, however, gaining agreement on precisely how to bring about simplification will not be easy.

Issues of pupil behaviour in some Scottish schools have received a great deal of attention in the media and the Executive wishes to "tackle discipline problems and bullying". There is no doubt that, for those pupils who are victims of bullying, the experience of schooling can be very unhappy and parents rightly demand that effective policies should be put in place. A few parents have resorted to legal action or have withdrawn their children and educate them at home. Most Scottish schools now have written anti-bullying policies but these do not guarantee effective enforcement as many instances of bullying take place outside the school gates or on school buses. Even where bullies are identified and evidence established, the process of suspending and excluding offenders can be complicated. Headteachers may be under pressure from local authorities not to exclude offenders and, in any case, even persistently badly behaved pupils have certain educational rights. The challenge is to find a way of making provision for such pupils, in the hope that they do not become completely alienated from learning, while protecting the right of the majority not to have their education constantly disrupted.

For some years, inspectorate reports have expressed concern about the transition between primary and secondary schools, particularly in respect of the under-achievement of boys in S1 and S2. Various explanations have been offered. It is claimed, for example, that the work is insufficiently challenging and does not take proper account of what has already been done in the upper primary school. The absence of male role models has been blamed: most teachers, secondary as well as primary, are now women and this occupational "feminisation" is thought to encourage a laddish anti-school sub-culture among some boys. Another explanation suggests that schools simply seem old-fashioned institutions. Compared to the worlds of sport, television and computer technology, schools can seem dull and this too has been cited as an explanation for resistance. One official response is to "have teachers work across primary and secondary schools" to try to ensure greater continuity in the learning experience of pupils. While this may be worth trying it seems a rather limited structural response to what is a much more deep-rooted cultural and institutional problem. Schools may need to change much more fundamentally than this.

Educating for Excellence also proposes to "strengthen the role of inspection". This is designed to give greater powers to deal with schools which are perceived to be failing to deliver high quality education. Again, the aim is a laudable one, intended to ensure that pupils and parents are well served. But what is the best way of proceeding? In England so-called "super heads", drafted in to save "failing schools", have not been a notable success, with some of them resigning after a very short time in post. Equally, too much reliance on a school's own self-evaluation of its strengths and weaknesses may lead to an inadequate response to deep-rooted problems. The inspectorate approach in the past has essentially been managerialist in character, setting targets and milestones which have to be reached within a specified time-frame. This may be part of the answer but so much of what goes on in a school cannot be reduced to a checklist, flow chart or development plan: it is about relationships and values and climate, qualities that are hard to define and pin down. Likewise, the leadership qualities of headteachers are important but to place all the responsibility on one person may simply deflect attention from the wider social and political context in which they are required to operate.

Towards an alternative policy agenda

In the run-up to devolution, much was promised in terms of a new approach to democracy. It was said that the Scottish Parliament would be more accessible, open and responsive than the old Scottish Office and that a more participative approach to policy-making would develop. The extent to which this has happened in education is questionable. There have certainly been plenty of "consultations" but these have been tightly managed by the civil service so that the outcome has been more influenced by traditional professional groups and existing bureaucratic institutions than by new voices. A major challenge for Scotland is to encourage new voices, not least those of young people themselves, who will question conventional ways of doing things and bring forward creative ideas.

This will not be easy because those who have been used to controlling the marketplace of ideas will fear a loss of control. An example will serve to illustrate the point. In September 2003 a review group was set up to consider the future of initial teacher education. In the ministerial statement which accompanied the announcement of the review, Peter Peacock said that he wanted the group to "think innovatively" and "consider proposals for radical change if that is what is needed". Unfortunately, neither the terms of reference nor the membership is likely to encourage radical thinking. No mention is made of the possibilities of inter-professional training whereby teachers, social workers and health service staff might receive part of their training together, addressing common issues in professionalism. This would be consistent with the claimed desire to encourage "joined up provision" of public services as one means of promoting greater social inclusion. As for the membership of the group, it consists of familiar beneficiaries of patronage: two directors of education, two deans of faculties of education, the registrar of the GTC, representatives of the Headteachers' Association of Scotland and the Educational Institute of Scotland – all under the watchful eyes of two senior civil servants. If there were a real commitment to change, one or two "wild cards" would have been included, such as a recent graduate of the existing courses or a person with expertise in training other occupational groups. Teacher education, in its present form, encourages and rewards conformity: it desperately needs an injection of new ideas.

Somewhat more promising is the review group that has been set up to look at the curriculum for the 3-18 age range. This has a broad remit and a membership that includes some people who have a track record of speaking their minds. Once again, however, it is headed by the same senior civil servant who is chairing the teacher education review, with the chief executive of LTS as vice-chair. Both are skilled at the "management of consent" and are likely to be more concerned with operational matters than with underlying curricular principles. The conditions for major reform of the curriculum are demanding: a sound philosophical rationale; openness to new thinking about knowledge, skills and learning; adequate resources; creative forms of staff development (as distinct from the "death by Powerpoint" approach); a willingness to challenge the vested interests of traditional groups within the system. To push a genuinely reforming agenda through will require good arguments, professional courage and strong political will.

The evidence of recent years suggests that the capacity of the Scottish educational establishment to reform itself is limited. That is why the contribution of external agencies to social and political thinking is vitally important. One of the positive features of post-devolution Scotland is the contribution that is being made by independent "think tanks" such as the Scottish Civic Forum, the Institute of Contemporary Scotland, the Scottish Council Foundation, Big Thinking and the Scottish Forum for Modern Government. The world of education can be narrow and inward-looking, and agencies which re-connect it with developments in wider society are highly valuable. The big issues of our time – globalisation, the knowledge economy, post-modern assaults on the concept of truth, the development of social capital, democratic renewal – have huge implications for the form and content of education at all levels. We need to ask ourselves a series of hard questions about the kind of society we currently have, the values that underpin it, and the contribution that education in its various forms can make to the kind of society we want in the future. This will require a longer-term view of policy than that which currently prevails. In a Scottish Council Foundation publication the question is posed: "Will the traditional concept of 'school' survive long into the twenty-first century"? Underlying this question are profound issues to do with the impact of technology, the pace of knowledge generation, the changing skills requirements of employers, and democratic demands for flexible forms of learning. At international level, there is a recognition of some of the implications. The

Organisation for Economic Cooperation and Development (OECD), for example, has developed six scenarios of future schooling which try to take account of social, cultural and economic forces on educational requirements. The scenarios range from modest adjustments to existing provision, through "re-schooling" alternatives, to "de-schooling" outcomes which envisage the collapse of traditional forms of schooling altogether.

In Scotland there is little evidence that such long-term, large-scale thinking is taking place within the political establishment. Our tradition is sceptical of grand theorising, preferring a modest pragmatic approach. But even here we are remarkably blind to what does not sit comfortably with our preferred view. Despite all the talk of social inclusion, the fact remains that some forty per cent of children in Glasgow live in poverty and are entitled to free school meals and clothing grants. Contrast this with the situation of Jordanhill School in the west end of the city, a school that does not come under local authority control but is funded directly by the Scottish Executive. So popular is it that house prices in the area attract fifty per cent and more above the asking price. In Edinburgh almost a quarter of the school-age population attend independent schools. It would be interesting to know how many children of senior civil servants, lawyers and other professionals are among their number. The fact remains that, despite all the "feel good" rhetoric about the Scottish tradition in education, allegedly underpinned by the principles of equality and democracy, Scotland is still, in many respects, a deeply divided society. As the radical educationist R. F. Mackenzie said in *The Unbowed Head* (1977): "Scotland's schools are at the centre of Scotland's perplexity, one of its main causes."

Part I: Estates of Scotland

Business and Economics

Gavin Reid

It is 1773. A lonely figure walks the desolate beach of the Lang Toune, Kirkcaldy. Darkly dressed, almost of clerical appearance, he is absorbed in thought. Mumbling to himself, walking awkwardly, he occasionally takes a lump of sugar from his pocket to crunch as he reflects. This is Adam Smith, founder of the concept of the market economy, and author-to-be of what is regularly cited as one of the most influential books ever written, *The Wealth of Nations* (1776). Economies, as Adam Smith recognised, serve social, political, military, ethical, cultural and many other purposes. True, they are institutions for allocating, and extending, a nation's resources, but they are much more than this. As I open to you my album of snapshots of the Scottish economy, I have Smith's sagacious work much in mind.

Time moves forward: the year is 1843. A young boy sits on the back of the horse-drawn cart, which his father is driving. It is loaded with family possessions, clothing, tools, utensils, furniture. He is crying bitterly. In front of him is the home he is leaving, a weaver's cottage in Dunfermline. His family have been evicted because of the radical views of his father, a weaver and convinced socialist, born into a Chartist tradition. Ahead of the boy is the road west, and then west again, on a sea journey, and beyond, to Pittsburgh in the USA. The boy's name is Andrew Carnegie. He was to go on to become the richest man on earth, and a great philanthropist. In 1892, the Carnegie Steel Company was valued at £25 million, making it the largest in the world. When this company was sold in 1901, for £400 million, this made Carnegie the richest man in the world.

Now it is 1993. A student is asleep in his office (his bedroom) when the doorbell rings. His mother comes to the door for him. She is worried about his studies in applied computing. His lecturers at Dundee University see he is gifted, but find he is straying from his studies, thinking of ways to market his ideas. He was the first student in Dundee University to use a mobile phone: he already looks like an entrepreneur. Within one year, he has moved his office out of the bedroom to a site in Dundee, then on to Dunfermline, and then back to the city he loves, Dundee. He is Chris van der Kuyl, founder-owner of Vis Interactive, a rising star in the global market for computer games, selling to mass markets such products as *Earthworm Jim*. Using his adage "rules are for fools", he recently hit his milestone targets of sales of £500 million and employment of 250 – taking him above the "small firms" classification.

We see that Scotland has deep roots as an enterprise economy. As a nation, we have produced, and do produce, great business figures. We have produced, and do produce, good economists, and business analysts. We have produced, and do produce, a skilled and well educated work force. We have produced, and do produce, world class innovations. Yet Chancellor Nigel Lawson famously mocked the Scottish economy in 1987 for not promoting the spirit of enterprise. Graham Ross, of Scottish Business in the Community retorted: "We ought to know how to run an enterprise economy – after all we invented it." Yet the criticism stung. Attitude surveys at the time indicated that entrepreneurship was a dirty word, rating very low in social status. At the top of the "status table" were the likes of lawyers, physicians and accountants.

By the end of the 1980s we confronted having to learn about entrepreneurship all over again. As I shall suggest below, we have done this difficult task quite well. And we do now have an economy which is actually performing rather well, and this against the tide of history, where "come back kids" in economic performance are known to be rare. Where is this economic reference point we need to come back to?

At the time of writing *The Wealth of Nations*, Adam Smith observed what he called "the general poverty" of his countrymen. He thought, as a consequence, that the Scots were "listless" compared to the English. Their economy had a poor resource base, and its markets needed liberalisation. Smith anticipated the emergence of the Industrial Revolution, and wrote of the rise of what he called the manufactory (factory), and the activities of projectors (entrepreneurs). However, he died in 1790 before it really got underway. By 1810, its effects were apparent, and both income per head and population had risen sharply. Smith's "manufactories" exploited the "division of labour" he had analysed in Chapter 1 of *The Wealth of Nations* to a marked degree. Yet even Smith would have been amazed by the success of the Scottish economy.

Essentially, this arose from the adoption of his economic ideas. Scottish energies seemed to be released, and with expanding markets, incomes rose, and poverty was diminished. Defunct mercantilist views, favouring the restriction of trade, were pushed aside, and a reforming spirit drove forward the new industrial and commercial order. This reforming spirit, which was based on a Calvinist ethic, seemed well suited to the emerging capitalist form of production, with its emphasis on parsimony and thrift. It was a cost-cutting, high-saving, high-investing, market-expanding, innovative, profit-orientated society that was emerging. It believed in education for all, and was willing to endorse enthusiastically one of the many exceptions that Smith recognised to private provision, namely the public provision of education.

The mood of the Victorian form of capitalism was well captured by the work of Samuel Smiles of Haddington, in a book, *Self Help*, of 1866, which became revered overseas, especially in Japan, when this country too chose to adopt a capitalist route, after the "Scottish Samurai", early merchant adventurers to distant foreign shores, had become vectors carrying the entrepreneurial spirit into that ancient culture. Margaret Thatcher, admittedly more a visceral than intellectual mind, in trying to revive the Victorian drive to economic success, as a way out of recession, often expressed her admiration of Smiles' work.

Scotland enjoyed great material progress in Victorian times. Between 1830 and 1900 the Scottish population increased from two and a half to four and a half million, much of it associated with a movement of labour off the land to the cities. Glasgow, the "Dear Green Place" of Gaelic legend, a beautiful, leafy cathedral city, a seat of ancient learning, with a fine fifteenth century university college, rather similar to Peterhouse College, Cambridge, and the sparkling River Kelvin flowing through it, abundant with salmon, was transformed. Over the same sixty-year period, Glasgow grew from half a million citizens to two million, a size greater than it is today. Another thirty years on, "The Dear Green Place" was no more than a distant memory. Even the industrial might of the "Second City of the Empire" was lost. Glasgow had become the "No Mean City" of the 1930s depression, a city blighted by the razor gangs of the Penny Mob, the Billy Boys and the Norman Conks. The bourgeois life of the West End was set against the gritty battle for survival in the Gorbals.

Against this trend to urbanisation, and urban disorder, Scotland was the first nation to introduce free banking, and the organisational form by which it flourished, namely branch banking. Between 1825 and 1914, the liabilities of Scottish banks rose from £11 per capita to £28 per capita. The commercial spirit was virile, exploratory and expansionist, and over the same period, Scottish foreign investment rose from £60 million to £500 million. Infrastructure improved greatly: roads, ports, canals, and railways, all that better promoted what Smith would have called the "carriage trade," the system of distribution, like the blood vessels of an increasingly muscular economy. The development of this industrial strength was associated with the rise of shipbuilding and engineering, the production of coal, iron and steel, the emergence of Scottish textiles, and the rise of other industrial activities, like chemicals, oils and spirits.

Of course, the vitality of the Victorian era was replaced by the complacence, and false dawn, of the Edwardian era, then the Great War, then the Great Depression, and finally the Second World War. These events had devastating consequences for the structure of the Scottish economy. Economically important to the war effort in each major conflict, by the mid-twentieth century Scotland had become over-specialised, too dependent on heavy industries, and distrustful of entrepreneurship. Its prospects looked bleak as the latter part of the twentieth century progressed. As a consequence of the creation of a planned war time economy (with great success, using free marketeers like Lionel Robbins, to do the planning), Britain took a long time to shake off the shackles of planning after the Second World War. We were slow to dismantle what Smith would have described as "mercantilist" restrictions of trade.

Though a post-war baby, I am old enough to remember rationing. Another snapshot, dated as late as 1952, is of me going an errand for my mother to the local grocer's store (no fears then of your nipper coming to grief), with ration tokens in my hand, for sugar. A later snapshot, at Aberdeen University, in my Junior Honours year, 1967-68, is of my econometrics lecturer, Jonathan St George Jephcote, producing a Labour Government consultancy report on, of all things, the future prospects of the furniture industry, as part of the National Plan. We had remained planners. The Scottish merchant sentiment, and our canny commercial instinct, had been lost, buried or suppressed, and needed re-discovering, even though the Second World War had became a distant memory.

Scottish economic policy, aimed at this re-discovery, has approached the stimulation of entrepreneurship in a variety of ways. My own view is that the enterprise system is a type of public good, in the same sense (as James Buchanan would say) that the work ethic is a public good. As such it has classical problems of provision by voluntary action alone. The state may need to be pro-active in ensuring such a system exists. The Small Industries Council for Rural Areas in Scotland (SICRAS) was one of the first institutional attempts to grapple with the problem of stimulating small enterprises, the life blood of entrepreneurship. This, and the Scottish Council (for Development and Industry), were part of the early post-World War Two piece-meal attempts at enterprise stimulation. These initiatives were part of a general indicative planning ethos, emphasising development boards and corporations. Public initiatives along these lines reached a high point when the Scottish Development Agency (SDA) was created in 1975. The SDA was of evolutionary design, betraying early roots in earlier institutional forms. For example, the functions of SICRAS were taken over by the Small Business Division of the SDA, with an extension of its remit to urban areas, and a beefing up of its ability to act as a small business advisory service. This unit alone displays the problems of an indicative planning approach. Its local offices flourished, and it was asked to provide finance capital, in both loan and equity forms, to promising projects that could not attract private sector support. The irony of the notion that rejected private projects needed public support was not lost on some civil servants, but not surprisingly it all ended in tears, with high loan losses, and the rate of return of investments over the period 1980-5 being negative.

In advancing its indicative planning aims, the SDA chose a number of "strategic sectors" as offering development potential: microelectronics, biotechnology, food processing, advanced engineering, textiles, and fashion. These are listed pretty much in the order of priority, and they by no means constitute a set of failures. However, Scottish textiles has been a loser, and fashion has not yet taken off in the way expected, though ambitions remain strong for success in this area, mainly focused on Edinburgh. Microelectronics and biotechnology have been relatively successful, food processing and advanced engineering less so, though the latter has enjoyed the stimulus of North Sea oil, and the opportunities for innovation in marine engineering.

However, as one disaggregate, the success stories are less obvious. This happens because sectors are not companies. The approach does not address the supply-side needs and the demand-side opportunities of individual companies. To put it in terms of modern theories of entrepreneurship, the sectoral planning approach lacks "time and place" information. The centre, which determines priorities, is too remote from ground operations, and when it acts can often be out of date. To reinforce this point, supply side needs, like specific labour skills, appropriate forms of finance, and suitable business premises, and so on, are often not sector-specific, but cross-sectoral in nature.

The form for enterprise stimulation that we have at the moment, Scottish Enterprise, emerged by private initiative. A Falkirk business man, Bill Hughes, obtained access to Downing Street by unconventional means, and managed to broker a meeting with Norman Fowler (then Secretary of State for Employment) at Chequers. At this meeting he directly "sold" the idea to Fowler of the "growth coalition", a regional development strategy that seemed to have produced the Massachusetts miracle. This approach focused on private, rather than public, sector leadership, and better training, targeted at the local level, right down to school level, if necessary. We did not have the Private Industry Councils (PICs) of Massachusetts, but we did have the Enterprise Trusts (ETs), highly localised enterprise stimulating units, numbering some fifty or so. Under Conservative policy, indicative planning died, and a new approach took over in 1988, harnessing these ETs, attenuating the centre (Scottish Enterprise National, as it was called), and introducing a new tier between the centre and the local level, the Local Enterprise Companies (LECs), numbering some dozen or so. The aim was to achieve eighty per cent delegation to the regions, and the LECs, largely managed by businessmen, would encourage appropriate training regimes, and control the budgets.

I have comparative evidence to suggest that this framework worked well for a while, say up to 1997. At present, there is a widespread feeling that the current framework is outmoded. In particular, the usefulness of the role of LECs is doubted. I agree with this, but do regret that the fallout of criticism has fallen heavily on the shoulders of the new Director, Robert Crawford, who inherited an outmoded organisation, and has not had sufficient time to re-structure, to meet the needs of a more knowledge based, information intensive economy.

Most controversial has been the business birth rate strategy of 1992, pioneered by the then Director, Crawford Beveridge, which aimed, within this Scottish Enterprise Framework, to bring Scotland up to the UK level on start ups. A great deal was achieved, with the business birth rate doubling between 1992 and 1995. However, recently the strategy has been judged a failure, for example in the writings of Professor Brian Ashcroft. On a visit to Cardiff, last December, a recent snapshot, I have been aghast to see that the Welsh Assembly is endorsing a commitment to a business birth rate strategy that is as ambitious (and unrealistic) as that adopted a decade ago by Scotland. Is this a win-win situation for consultants who get paid to encourage unrealistic goals, and then come back and offer further advice, when it all goes pear-shaped?

I agree that, statistically, Scotland still is not a top performer in small firm formation, but would balance that against other considerations. Above all, the entrepreneurial climate is utterly different from when I first started field work on new businesses back in 1984. It was uncommon for there to be a business plan at start up, and few small businesses used ITC clusters. Also, few of the business founders I met displayed an entrepreneurial spirit. For many, the push factor (e.g. redundancy, long-term unemployment) was predominant.

Some of my most recent snapshots of the Scottish economy have been obtained as I tracked 150 start-up businesses over a five-year period, using a representative sample stretching from Inverurie, down to Edinburgh, then across to Glasgow, and out into Lanarkshire. The increase in business competence is palpable since the mid eighties. Further, the evidence on quality of start up is relatively favourable in Scotland: they tend to last longer, and therefore have more impact on the local economy, in terms of continuity of employment, the spreading of entrepreneurial skills and attitudes, and the encouraging of family succession. Not only is the evidence of entrepreneurship visible in most new businesses, it has now permeated all levels of education, from primary schools to universities. Chris van der Kuyl is now a folk hero to youngsters on Tayside.

Today, thanks partly to the activities of such "new" entrepreneurs, Scotland has the profile of a very modern economy. It is largely a thriving, service-based (education, health, social, financial, business) economy, but has high quality manufacturing and construction capabilities, a small but efficient primary sector, and a public sector which seems somewhat larger (relatively) than England's, but smaller by comparison with many EU neighbours. It has a well educated workforce, excellent universities, high innovative capabilities, and a flexible labour market. We worry about matters like fiscal devolution, converting our innovative potential into commercial products, and the falling population (a combination of a declining net reproductive rate and economic emigration). However, it was perhaps no surprise that two recent economics gurus flown into Scotland from Princeton University, Professors Baumol and Krugman, for the Allander series of talks, in Edinburgh and Glasgow, both gave us a relatively encouraging, if not clean, bill of economic health. We are not top of the rankings, but we do well on several measures of entrepreneurship, against sensible comparison nations, like Ireland, Finland, Denmark, Norway, and New Zealand. Further, the evidence from Donald MacRae is that our universities are efficient and effective at innovation. Obviously we need to improve on the volume and value of innovative activity.

The organiser of the Allander series, Wendy Alexander, now a professor at Strathclyde University, was until recently Minister of Enterprise, Transport, and Lifelong Learning – a very broad (and heavy) portfolio to carry. It is a serious loss to policy making in this area that she felt unable to continue in this post. I recall a speech she made in May 2002 in which she asked us to be "a hotbed of technological innovation," no doubt deliberately paraphrasing Smollett, over two centuries earlier, talking of the "hotbed of genius" that was the Scottish Enlightenment. That May, she referred to Scotland as being third in the world for scientific citations, with world standing in a number of technologies, including life sciences, optoelectronics and microelectronics. Amongst the firms she mentioned were Cyclacel in Dundee and Strakan in Galashiels.

Before writing this final draft, late in October 2003, I checked the current performance of these companies. Cyclacel, which develops modern therapeutics for cancer, had just announced a word agreement with the MRC for worldwide distribution of Drosophila (RNAi); and Strakan, a developer of new drugs for bone and skin disease, had just received a European Patent Office grant of patent for an anti-microbial product, covering its core technology.

The bed may not yet be hot, but it is warming up.

Part I: Estates of Scotland

Law

Robert Black

For the health of a legal system there are two things that are absolutely essential. The first of these requirements is a properly functioning legislature where elected representatives of the population served by and subject to the system can oversee the operation and monitor the content of the system and can make changes where change is required. The administration of the law as well as its content and substance must always be kept under democratic scrutiny with a view to reform. These are matters that are much too important to the general health of any society to be left to lawyers. The second essential is a properly functioning system of courts where judges who have, and who (through their manner of appointment and their conditions of tenure of office) deserve to have, the confidence of the population, administer criminal justice and adjudicate upon civil claims and disputes. Without such legislative and judicial institutions I would suggest that a society cannot truly be described as civilised. Prior to the implementation of the devolution settlement in 1999 it can be convincingly demonstrated that we in Scotland did not have the first of these essential prerequisites. And it is eminently arguable that it is only through the post-1999 actions of devolved institutions that we are at long last beginning to have the second.

Since the devolved Parliament and Executive provided for in the Scotland Act 1998 came into being during 1999, we now have a locally-based legislature which, amongst many other functions, can keep our legal system and the administration of justice under review. This is of itself a major advance. The former position whereby Scottish legislation was dependent upon time being found in a UK parliament, eighty-five per cent of whose members had no connection with or interest in the affairs of Scotland, was quite simply intolerable and unacceptable. Necessary and urgent reforms in the substance of the law and in the administration of justice were delayed, sometimes for years, until governmental inclination in Whitehall and parliamentary time at Westminster could be found. And when eventually time was found, the legislation often took the form of a Law Reform (Miscellaneous Provisions) (Scotland) Bill: a rag-bag of wholly unconnected topics each of which, in England, would have been the subject of a separate Bill and have received separate scrutiny. Alternatively, Scottish provisions might be tacked on as a sort of afterthought to legislation that had been drafted with the needs of the English legal system in mind: the dreaded "application to Scotland" clause.

There were some Scottish lawyers who thoroughly approved of this state of affairs on the basis that the law and legal system of Scotland were in consequence largely left to their own devices and kept out of the clutches of meddling politicians, however well-meaning. For them benign neglect was infinitely preferable to rigorous parliamentary scrutiny. Developments took place, if at all, slowly and incrementally through decisions of the Scottish courts. The levers of legal change rested firmly in the hands of lawyers, particularly judges, who could always be relied upon to do nothing that would frighten the horses. All very cosy.

Now we have a Scottish Parliament that takes an active interest in justice, legal affairs and the legal system in Scotland. Indeed, such is the politicians' interest in these subjects and such is the volume of work, that the Scottish Parliament quickly found it necessary to have not one but two Justice Committees operating simultaneously, the only area of the Parliament's business in which this has happened. I take the liberty to suggest that at least one important reason why there is so much work for the Parliament in the justice area is the decades of neglect from which it suffered under the Westminster and Whitehall regime.

The Parliament through its legislation has already been responsible for important developments affecting the administration of justice in Scotland. One example of this is the changes that came into force on 1 November 2002, greatly restricting the circumstances in which the sexual history of the complainer in a rape trial can be ventilated, and introducing potentially very serious consequences indeed for an accused person (disclosure to the jury of his own previous convictions) if he succeeds in bringing such material before the court (Sexual Offences (Procedure and Evidence) (Scotland) Act 2002. Following the passing of the Criminal Justice (Scotland) Act 2003 further far reaching changes in criminal evidence, procedure and sentencing entered into operation on 27 June 2003. In addition major alterations in the rules for taking evidence in civil and criminal court proceedings from children and other potentially vulnerable witnesses are likely in the near future under the Vulnerable Witnesses (Scotland) Bill introduced on 23 June 2003. These reforms would, under the old dispensation, either not have taken place at all or have taken place only years later when they could be squeezed into the Westminster parliamentary programme.

When circumstances necessitate it, the Scottish Parliament can act very speedily indeed to rectify a problem which has suddenly emerged. For example, a serious problem in the operation of the summary (non-jury) criminal procedure system was disclosed by a decision of the High Court of Justiciary handed down on 14 February 2002. The implication was that hundreds, if not thousands, of summary criminal cases proceeding through the system would be brought to an abrupt conclusion and never come to trial. The Scottish Parliament acted to amend the relevant criminal procedure legislation to prevent this undesirable consequence, and the resulting Bill had passed through all its parliamentary stages and received the royal assent by 8 March 2002, some three weeks after the difficulty first emerged. Had we still been dependent upon the Westminster Parliament for legislation to address the problem, I can confidently assert that amending legislation would not have been enacted by today and in all probability not for several years from today.

The Scottish Parliament has, of course, been the target of a protracted campaign of scathing criticism in the tabloid press (in which category I personally place the *Scotsman* which, while broadsheet in format, has become resolutely tabloid in editorial and journalistic values). Such criticism has often, in my view, been based on a failure (in many cases probably wilful) to differentiate between the Scottish Executive and the Scottish Parliament. However that may be, and however the Parliament (as distinct from the Executive) may be judged to have performed in other subject areas there can be no doubt that in the performance of its function of oversight and, where necessary, reform of the justice system, it has been a runaway success.

Thus, devolved government has supplied us with the first of the essential preconditions of a viable modern legal system, namely an operative legislature. And this is something that, in the area of the administration of justice, I resolutely contend that the Westminster model signally failed to provide.

But what of my second essential, a system of courts staffed by judges who, by virtue of their manner of appointment and their conditions of tenure of office, would have to be regarded by any objective and fair-minded observer as independent and impartial dispensers of justice? It is my contention that the court system inherited by the Scottish Executive in 1999 did not pass this test. This may be thought to be a surprising, perhaps even an outrageous, claim for me to make. But in one respect at least it is a claim that quite clearly must be accepted by even the most die-hard supporter of the old pre-devolution regime.

At the time of devolution a distressingly high proportion of the criminal business in Scotland's Sheriff Courts (around thirty per cent) was in the hands not of permanent full-time sheriffs but of persons holding temporary part-time appointments (normally for one year at a time) from the Secretary of State for Scotland. Cantankerous people like me had for years been publicly complaining that this was constitutionally improper. We pointed out that a crucial element in the concept of judicial independence was that the tenure of office of judges should accord them freedom both in actuality and in public perception from political pressure and external political influence in any decision which they might be called upon to take. Temporary sheriffs had no security of tenure. They held office technically at the pleasure of the Secretary of State for Scotland (though in reality at the pleasure of the Lord Advocate).

The oath which all judges must swear requires them to act "without fear or favour, affection or ill will". A fair-minded observer might well ask how acting without fear or favour could be accomplished and, more importantly, could be seen to be accomplished when the temporary sheriff was dependent for his continuance in office upon the will of the legal politician, namely the Lord Advocate, who (or whose local representative) is a party to virtually every criminal case that every temporary sheriff was ever required to adjudicate upon. It therefore came as no surprise to me when, within six months of the incorporation into domestic law of the European Convention on Human Rights simultaneously with the coming into operation of the devolution settlement, temporary sheriffs were held not to be an independent and impartial tribunal as required under the fair trial provisions of article six of the European Convention. And so, at a stroke, temporary sheriffs ceased to exist or, at least, to be competent to sit in criminal proceedings. So there you have one incontrovertible instance of the pre-devolution Scottish judicial system not matching up to the essential, minimum, internationally recognised standards for an acceptable system of administration of justice.

But surely, you will be thinking, there were no other major defects or flaws in the Scottish judicial system inherited by the new regime. Well, actually, there were. And the principal remaining flaw might be thought to be a really quite fundamental one. It related to the crucial issue of the general procedure for the appointment of all full-time Scottish judges, whether at Supreme Court (that is Court of Session and High Court) level or Sheriff Court level. When the devolution settlement came into operation in 1999 the situation regarding the appointment of judges in both the Supreme Court and the Sheriff Court was that nomination rested in the hands of the Lord Advocate. He it was who selected the candidate whose name would be passed by the First Minister (by the Secretary of State for Scotland before devolution) to the Queen. This was, and always had been, a constitutional outrage. The Lord Advocate, among other functions, is the head of the Scottish centralised system of prosecution of crime. With only the rarest and most trivial of exceptions, every prosecution in Scotland is brought in his name or in the name of his local representative, the procurator fiscal. He is accordingly party to virtually every case heard in every criminal court in Scotland. How then could it possibly be seriously contended that the High Court of Justiciary and the Sheriff Court in exercising criminal jurisdiction were independent and impartial tribunals when their judges had without exception been appointed to their office by one of the litigants, namely the prosecutor?

This has now been rectified through the establishment by the Scottish Executive of an independent judicial appointments board which is responsible for selecting the name which the First Minister will then present to the Queen for appointment to a vacant judicial position. Never let it be thought, however, that the Lord Advocate ceded his powers of patronage without a struggle. In the consultation document on the subject distributed by the Scottish Executive Justice Department in April 2000, *Judicial Appointments: An Inclusive Approach,* what was proposed was that the new independent selection board should simply vet the suitability of candidates for judicial office, with the right of nomination to fill the actual vacancy, from among those found suitable by the board, being left in the hands of the Lord Advocate.

Fortunately, this little ruse was sufficiently transparent to be detected and countered by a number of those who responded during the consultation exercise (including the former Lord Justice Clerk, Lord Ross and, much less importantly, myself). But it is, perhaps, instructive to note that a group of existing High Court judges in their joint response to the consultation document saw no constitutional impropriety or conflict of interest in the Lord Advocate's traditional role in the appointment of judges and urged that it was important that his input should continue. This might not, at first blush, have seemed calculated to inspire public confidence in the ability of these judges to identify and adjudicate upon issues, such as the fair trial provisions (including those relating to the independence and impartiality of judges) which it falls upon them to decide under the, then, newly-incorporated European

Convention on Human Rights.

Some judges even seem to be in a state of denial that the Lord Advocate did in fact nominate them for appointment under the bad old regime. But as the consultation document, and the response by Lord Ross, mentioned in the last paragraph make clear, there really is absolutely no doubt on the matter. Further corroboration is available in *Lord Advocate's Diary 1961-1966* by Gordon Stott (Aberdeen University Press, 1991), particularly pages 161 to 177 where the Lord Advocate in Harold Wilson's first government entertainingly outlines the machinations involved in his nomination of several sheriffs and judges, including especially his then Solicitor-General, James Leechman.

The new Scottish judicial appointments system is, I am satisfied, Convention compliant. But what of still-serving judges who were appointed by the Lord Advocate of the day under the now superseded bad old system? Would they, if challenged, be held to be independent and impartial in criminal cases in which one of the parties was, as he always is, the Lord Advocate? I confess that I have my doubts (though it may be that the terms of their employment would be held sufficiently to guarantee their independence and impartiality and so outweigh the deficiencies in the manner of their original appointment). Inevitably, however, the issue will be raised one of these days before the Judicial Committee of the Privy Council in London under the Scotland Act or before the European Court of Human Rights in Strasbourg. I would not place money on the outcome. But at least it can be said that the Scottish Executive, within three short years of coming into existence, rectified, for the future, an obvious and inexcusable blot on the administration of justice in Scotland and one that for over two hundred years no United Kingdom government had seen fit to tackle.

It is accordingly my contention that as regards the essentials, the fundamentals, of the administration of justice, the Scottish Parliament and the Scottish Executive have, in a manner and to an extent unmatched by their predecessor institutions, been providing to the people of Scotland what justice requires.

Part I: Estates of Scotland

Religion

R D Kernohan

I have never found anything so hard to write as this chapter and have wondered why. It can't merely be because I'm at odds with so many fellow Scots for whom religious observance and its only true begetter, religious belief, play no vital part in life. I never feel so blate about matters, including politics, in which I may be in a smaller minority. There may be an element in my reluctance of an uncertainty, which unsettles other believing sinners too, perhaps most acutely in a country with a religious inheritance as significant as Scotland's. How far are we prisoners of grace, and how far creatures of old and diminishing habit?

When I was younger I sometimes envied those, like a majority of Scots today, who had not been predestined to a "Church background". They could exercise their free will either through joyful discovery of faith or in indifference with neither repining nor regret. I don't envy them now, for they struggle to understand so much in Scottish history and character that makes us what we are.

In modern Scotland, whatever we may believe about the continuing power of grace, the influence of religion is much diminished, even if (as Church publicists sometimes insist) more people still go to church than to football matches. There's little consolation in comparisons with a league which has only two really strong congregations. Religion is alive but irregular in heartbeat, lacking in vigour, and inclined to bouts of uncertainty and depression.

The sociological background is to be found not only in the 2001 census figures, which show both the growth of irreligion and the gap between nominal religious adherence and Church involvement, but other league tables of civil marriages, baptisms, and admissions to full church membership. Take into account estimates of declining church attendance in recent decades, especially in the Church of Scotland and Roman Catholic Church. Or look at such less conventional indices as the sparse and sometimes esoteric "religion" sections of general bookshops and the almost complete absence of religious stipulations in the burgeoning newspaper-advertising from those seeking friendships, relationships, even conceivably marriages.

It wouldn't have happened in my young days. If we'd had those contact columns then, it would have been: "Cuddly, cute, bubbly redhead seeks Catholic for fun nights in/out". Or perhaps: "Broad-minded man would like to meet buxom similar lady, no strings (age, looks unimportant; Protestants only). Today's aspirants for "friendship, possibly more" seem astonishingly ecumenical in outlook. Even the occasional ethnic declaration – Asian man, Oriental lady, or whatever – seems indifferent to whether the candlelit dinner will involve pork chops, rib-roast, or the vegetarian option. Far more advertisers stipulate about smoking than religion, though I did find one "Christian" seeking fun times with an authoritative lady.

But I think the real reason for my reluctance to pontificate is a sense of inadequacy. That is not a statement of false modesty but of two practical difficulties. The more obvious one, at least to any believer, is that true assessments of any country's religious condition must draw on the data banks of Heaven, to which we are all currently denied access. The less obvious one, though derived from the truth behind that flashy epigram, is that as a believer becomes more conscious of the complexities, contradictions, occasional uncertainty or blessed assurance of his own faith he becomes less sure how these elements are mixed in others, even those with whom he recites the Creed or shares the Sacrament. We know what they adhere to but not how they have reached that belief or hold to it. Maybe the commonest condition now is one summed up by John Buchan: "Dogmatism gives way to questioning and questioning in the end to prayer." Besides, the beginning of wisdom in this matter recognises that much religious faith in Scotland, however ill defined or dependent more on instinct than intellect, survives among people who no longer go to church or perhaps never went. Some of it may be linked to New Age and similar tendencies or found in what (until the world's peoples and ideas became more jumbled together) seemed "Eastern" religions. Much more is linked, however loosely, to the one which came from the Middle East via Whithorn and Iona.

But an inevitable consequence is that religious institutions are forced into defensive or conciliatory postures. They organise rearguard actions against ultra-secularist tendencies, defend themselves against village atheists employed as newspaper columnists, and seek common ground and good causes in which many allies have no religious motivation or belief. None of these actions, some inspired by reason and others by reflexes, is wrong or unworthy, but they encourage analysis of religious conditions guided by sociology and media values. But, as I hope the bishop said to the actress, I recognise the power of these temptations but propose to resist them.

The sociological approach to religion is not to be despised and wholly rejected. It explains much about religion's role in shaping a country's institutions, values, and culture. It can reveal much about residual strength as well as social, habitual, or institutional decline of religion. But by its nature it concentrates on change and decay and only to a limited extent sees a need to explain the survival of religious beliefs in a cold climate. It is not its business, faced with fashionable dislike of "organised" or "institutional" religion, to examine the imperatives for religious organisation, or Christian beliefs about the divine institution as well as human fallibility of the Church. If Presbyterian ministers neither value nor even know the great passages of the Westminster Confession on the nature of the visible and invisible Church or the fallibility of Church institutions, one can hardly expect sociologists and journalists to be better informed.

Even less do I use "media values" as a term of reproach. If the Church today produced Old Testament prophets, even New Testament prophets like George MacLeod, Billy Graham, or Tom Allan, they would make their impact. Skilful statesmen of the

Church like Andrew Herron or Cardinal Winning never lacked column-inches. But it's the nature of media coverage to value what's likely to appeal to most readers, and most easily simplified – occasionally (as in coverage of Fundamentalism and Highland ultra-Calvinism) most easily caricatured. That concentrates attention on sex, controversies, and clerical delinquencies and, since news media must search for what's new, such novelties as a "woman-elder Moderator" and a "liberal" Cardinal from Scotland. I do not complain but try, as Paul advised the Galatians, to gently set right those who go astray. Media values produce elements of distortion when they give the impression that most Anglicans are obsessed with homosexuality, the average Presbyterian with reports of the Church and Nation Committee, or Scottish Roman Catholicism with nuances of its new Cardinal's opinions.

A weakness of much contemporary analysis of religious trends is that it insists on assessing them not by their intrinsic or spiritual significance but by whether they can be accommodated to whatever consensus our times can muster in politics, economics, sexual morals, and social responsibility. A large part of the Church, inclined to the same consensus, is complicit in the process. For it is always difficult for the Christian, necessarily committed to work for moral, social, and political order even in this world, to distinguish between what's enduring and essential and what is transient.

Such pressure is nothing new. It has been a constant factor in Church history since the Emperor Constantine made Christianity the State religion and it has invoked divine blessing on such passing fashions as feudalism, nationalism, the divine right of kings, *laissez-faire* economics, Socialism, and even (for some pliant or corrupted Churchmen) Communism and dictatorship of the proletariat. Today it manifests itself as an attempt to accommodate the Church to a general theory of liberalism and universal democracy with far more emphasis on human rights than the chief end of man.

That tendency is evident in the presentation and perception of what, on any scale of media values, is important recent events in Scottish religion. One is the elevation of Archbishop O'Brien to

Cardinal at a time when the college is likely soon to face a crucial, unpredictable decision and an equally unpredictable aftermath. The tendency has also been apparent during Pope John Paul's twenty-five years in Rome. Although hardly a liberal in politics and economics, his role in Eastern Europe aligned him with the greatest liberation movement of our age, and it was easy for secular liberal media to canonise him in his lifetime. But because he has been ultra-conservative in moral and especially sexual matters, sometimes right and sometimes quite wrong by my judgments, he encountered concealed but intense hostility. And on theological matters to which the secular establishment is indifferent – for example his emphasis on devotion to the mother of Jesus and his very Polish view of relations with Eastern Orthodoxy – there has been little critical assessment.

Cardinal O'Brien has suffered similar treatment in our Scottish ecclesiastical kailyard. I am a detached enough observer to guess ways in which seniority, differing personal merits, and varying emphases in opinion must have weighed on the Roman selection board, as well as to wonder whether Archbishop Conti is as ultra-conservative and Cardinal O'Brien as liberal as our media suggest. Secular journalists find it hard to grasp the idea that the Roman Church gives its people, even its princes, wide scope for intellectual speculation about faith and order, never mind such mere regulations as the celibacy imposed on its main body of priests, as distinct from Uniates and a few wandered ex-Anglicans.

What is crucial and still divides Christendom (or so it seems to me as a Protestant) is the firmness and structure of its imposed authority and its demand for obedience. I am not being critical of Cardinal O'Brien when I suggest that some of his quoted "liberal" opinions really display considerable authoritarian conservatism on such matters as inter-communion and enforced clerical celibacy. Freedom to think goes with submission to authority. For example, in the *Sunday Herald* (October 19, 2003), he makes the reasonable but not irrefutable debating point that "clergy of other denominations are allowed to get married and they are exactly the same as ourselves: short of ministers and priests". Other Christians simply do not think in terms of allowing any men and women to exercise a biblical and natural right. The historic thirty-nine Articles of the Church of England speak for us, declaring that all Christians may "marry at their own discretion, as they shall judge the same to serve better to godliness." The liberal Cardinal (as he is in some respects) not surprisingly shows some very traditional and deep-rooted assumptions about the authority of the institution he serves. Like many Roman Catholics he may be saddened by inability to share in the Lord's Supper with Protestants, but he is not one of the few who turn a right to think into defiance of regulations. Indeed, one of the ironies in this situation is that it is his critics on Catholicism's far Right who most vividly exercise a rather Protestant style in asserting the right of private judgment.

And so, keeping the best till last, to the belated nomination of a woman to be Moderator of the General Assembly of the Church of Scotland. The nomination of Dr Alison Elliot is good, wise, and welcome, but neither a world-shaking nor even a Kirk-shaking event. It shows style and image catching up with the substance of recent and continuing change in a Church which has faults enough and to spare but has always sought to be truly reforming as well as a true Reformed Church. A woman Moderator from Greyfriars Kirk of the National Covenant represents continuity and tradition as well as innovation. But in some ways an outstanding elder's nomination is more important than a woman's, for it will help the whole Church reflect how ministry is shared and collective authority exercised.

I don't devalue or disparage these events, which make their impact on secular media and secularised society, even if some media reaction is superficial and some insultingly ignorant, such as the claim that Dr Elliot will preside over the Church "founded by John Knox." However it is wise to set such media occasions in the true context of faith (to use William Barclay's rendering from Hebrews) as "the confidence that the things which as yet we only hope for really do exist. It is the conviction of the reality of the things which as yet are out of sight".

As John Buchan wrote in face of the Nazi and Communist pseudo-religions of his time: "Religion is born when we accept the ultimate frustrations of mere human effort and at the same time realise the strength which comes from union with superhuman reality". Modern Scotland might also remember his warning that "the Faith is an anvil which has worn out many hammers", but with the emphasis on three factors especially relevant to our own times.

The first emphasis must be on the extent to which Scottish religion, for all its distinctive and even picturesque historical characteristics, reflects the moods and condition of the Western Christendom to which it belongs. Despite the high regard I have for the editor-publisher of this book, I cannot unreservedly fulfil his instruction that this essay should be "essentially Scottish in orientation". Christianity in Scotland is no more "essentially Scottish" than our leaven of Judaism and new enclaves of Islam. The destiny of Scottish Christianity, so influenced by events in Wittenberg, Geneva, or Rome (and in Karl Barth's day in Barmen and Basel), is bound up with the dilemmas of the Church in "Old Europe" and with its turbulent, vigorous, untidy growth in the rest of the world.

This is not an age in which Western humanity is much inclined to accept its frustrations and limitations, or to concepts of the superhuman. The decline of "habitual religion" evident in Scotland does not greatly differ in mood or scale from that of Western Europe generally. Religion is alive but its pulse is rather weak – almost certainly weaker than in the United States or in Eastern Europe. Beyond the old Iron Curtain it has had what may be a temporary boost from new freedom and reaction against Marxism, and a more permanent one from recognition of the vital role of religious tradition in shaping national character. But in the future global trends may be as important as national character, and Western Europe may need more faith in face of worldwide turbulence.

The second emphasis must be on the tenacity of religious institutions, even when they are unfashionable and their influence, like their scale of activity, is diminished. That is evident in countries, Roman Catholic as well as Protestant in background, where the spiritual temperature and attendance at worship are probably appreciably lower than in contemporary Scotland. Even here it should be apparent (not least from the failure of the latest and less than fervent attempts to cobble together a united Protestant

Church) that institutions have a tenacious sense of identity, all the stronger when reinforced by a belief that they are emphasising or defending some important truth. Of course the demographic structure of the main denominations in Scotland, especially of the communicant rolls of the Church of Scotland and of the priesthood in the Roman Catholic Church, suggests that further symptoms of decline will be evident for some time. But they do not diminish the intensity of religious experience in Word and Sacrament for hundreds of thousands of Scots, and they go with a continuing response to pastoral care in times of trouble. These symptoms also obscure the vigour of very many congregations, inside and beyond the larger denominations. It is possible that in the near future this contrast between numerical decline and local or sectional vigour may become even more marked.

The third but most cautious emphasis must be on the self-evident truth that religious interest and even religious belief cannot be measured solely by the vigour or otherwise of Churches and other religious associations. (I think "faith communities" was the preferred term when I last paid any attention to political correctness.) I advise caution because I find that in this vast and only partially explored territory the apologists for both religion and secularism make too much of the evidence that suits them, or at least read it in the distorting light of their own hopes for the future. Too many ministers find solace in the hope that the moral impulses behind good causes, and more controversial Green ones, reflect a "new interest in spirituality" which will eventually refresh the Church. And I distrust people (like those who helped weaken religious education and the Christian culture of non-denominational schools and now attack the Roman Catholic sector) who profess to encourage a free market in religious ideas and moral discussion but do not conceal their pleasure at the decline of "organised religion".

The fairest assessment today is that institutional religion in Scotland is often rather disorganised, probably because of the extent to which the largest denominations, and especially the Church of Scotland, struggle to provide channels of grace for more people than want to use them. They arrange good works on a shoestring budget, struggle to tackle social needs which the public sector cannot meet, and offer pastoral care which most people can want only a little of the time. The predominant ethos of the Kirk, for example, is hostile to the idea of "gathered congregations" though part of its evangelical wing and several vigorous smaller denominations work effectively in this way. But its strength is unequal to the task of reinvigorating the parish system, whether on its own or in ad hoc ecumenical partnerships which make more sense than schemes for "organic union".

It isn't surprising that these religious institutions, shaped in social and intellectual environments very different from today's, cannot muster the sound and fury to bring the walls of our modern Jerichos tumbling down. To agnostic sociologists they must seem mere skeletons, with the landscape of Scotland littered with the dry bones of once-thriving churches. But some of us remember earlier prophecies about how dry bones will live. We still encounter those whose faith and good works show what "institutional religion" really is. And now and again we meet or hear of those who have only recently shared a walk to Emmaus and can tell us, with a freshness we may have lost, how their hearts burn within them.

Part I: Estates of Scotland

Medicine

Duncan Davidson

Nye Bevan said in Parliament in 1948, at the start of the National Health Service: "We are still able to do the most civilised thing in the world – put the welfare of the sick in front of every other consideration." How is the "welfare of the sick" faring fifty-five years later? Does the government still put their welfare first, and did it ever? This Labour government, apparent inheritors of Mr Bevan's vision, has conflicting agendas. Many others are responsible for the sick too. The medical professions, in the midst of many scientific and clinical developments, are subject to continuous administrative change and legal threat. Pharmaceutical companies have massive investments in health, with the potential for great profits and losses, while private practice has its own obvious interests and the media usually sells the drama of life, death and controversy. Whereas the focus of all this should be you, me, our relatives, and the rest of the population, the ill and the potentially ill.

Rising expectations for health are mixed with fear and helplessness. Little was expected when life was short, more people died of infection than cancer or heart disease, and trauma was often complicated by fatal infection. Now if we are smashed in a car accident we seek immediate effective professional care. But TV programmes and newspapers show images of chaotic, overworked casualty departments filled with demanding drunks. New symptoms puzzle us: could they be the start of a dread disorder that needs prompt diagnosis, or merely trivial, transient problems perhaps related to our own lifestyle? Several pages of printouts from a confusing Internet search, a telephone call to a remote medical call centre or a ten-minute consultation with the GP may not relieve the fears. Skilled professionals should treat that dreadful, nagging, painful hip promptly in a clean, pleasant supportive hospital. We hear, however, that waiting lists are interminable, that privatised cleaning services are poor and "bank" nurses, ignorant of the team, are brought in as stop-gaps. People with chronic disorders such as arthritis, multiple sclerosis, epilepsy and diabetes may seek to understand their illness, sometimes learning more than their paternalistic caring professionals. But the child, the frail, the institutionalised elderly, the mentally disturbed, and those with learning difficulties cannot express their needs. The critically ill often cannot make their own decisions and prefer to trust the staff. So who speaks for the patient?

The medical charities and voluntary organisations articulate these needs most clearly but they vary. They may speak for low-profile disorders, meeting in small, unhappy self-selected groups, often in cold church halls to provide support for each other and try to publicise their needs which go unrecognised by government and the media. Others, with emotive disorders like muscular dystrophy or representing common problems such as heart disease and cancer, have expanded. They raise money for research and have well-presented publications. Some charities realise that improved health services are essential; they lobby parliament, develop special interest groups among MSPs, negotiate with health boards, and participate as the voice of the patient in the development of new clinical guidelines.

The government for its part has a series of unsolved dilemmas. "Prudent" economy conflicts with spending commitments. "Health" is a political issue that talks of equity, availability and quality. Bevan was optimistic in his drive to create the NHS. An early idea was that with universal provision of "free" healthcare the population would become healthier and that the costs of healthcare would diminish. Some hope! Bevan could not have foreseen the explosive development of new treatments nor their costs. The Scottish Executive now has big plans. It promises to increase spending from £6.7 billion to £9.3 billion in the next parliament. Glossy brochures describe "Working together for a Healthy, Caring

Scotland." There is a raft of changes and new structures. NHS hospital trusts are to be replaced by unified NHS boards, there is to be support for innovation with a Change and Innovation Fund and a new health improvement challenge, community health partnerships, a Scottish Health Council, new complaints procedures, together with guarantees on waiting lists and clinical and local targets. Does this make you breathless with excitement? But it is administrative rather than clinical changes which are driving much of this agenda. A quotation attributed, with some dispute, to a Roman, Caius Petronius in AD 66, should be emblazoned across the walls of all administrators for it aptly summarises the effects of continued, ill-thought-out change:

"We trained hard but it seemed that every time we were beginning to form up into teams we would be reorganised. I was to learn later in life that we tend to meet any new situation by reorganising, and a wonderful method it can be for creating the illusion of progress while producing confusion, inefficiency and demoralisation."

Mrs Thatcher's government increased the expectations of the National Health Service. Statements of the rights of people to have prompt and effective treatment were displayed in waiting rooms for all to read as they waited and waited. Collective planning for health was destroyed in an attempt to replicate the marketplace with the separation of purchasers, the health boards, from the providers, the primary healthcare and the hospital trusts. Administrative costs increased. The Conservative government also promoted healthcare priorities and waiting times to measure success in certain key areas. More generally, there emerged the idea that individuals can promote their own aspirations without responsibility for others in the community. The government tried to suppress a major report on inequalities in health, the Black report, in 1980. It emphasised inequities and the social background of health. New Labour now enthusiastically continues with targets, perhaps in the hope that success in simple measures will demonstrate to the electorate how much they care. Measurement of outcomes in medicine is sensible and to be welcomed but selecting a few priorities distorts the broad range of issues. The current health priorities are cardiovascular disease, cancer and mental health but not others such as severely incapacitating neurological disorders.

And now there is the strange idea of PFI (Public Finance Initiative) for new buildings. A simple measure of the sense of PFI would be this. Government ministers, including the Minister of Health in Scotland, Malcolm Chisholm, should all live in their homes under PFI. Instead of borrowing the money for a house (or hospital) by a mortgage or loan they should enter into agreement with a private landlord to build a house (or hospital) for them. The landlord will minimise costs by designing it with the least number and smallest bedrooms possible, employing the cheapest methods. Mr Chisholm and others would then pay substantial rent. Their domestic services would be contracted out. The landlord would still own the property and still be the landlord at the end of the agreed term, say thirty years. When government ministers start living in their PFI homes, then the taxpayer and patients may be reassured that it is sensible. Meanwhile, criticism of the design and the costs of the "flagship" PFI development in the new Royal Infirmary of Edinburgh and others will continue with attacks on their design and on their running and long-term costs. Poor planning continues. A recent example in Edinburgh is the planning for major trauma. If you have a terrible accident in Edinburgh you will be taken to the trauma centre in the Royal Infirmary. If that trauma includes a head-injury requiring urgent neurosurgery, the base for that is in the Western General Hospital on the other side of the city. Drive carefully.

New government money, we are told, will pay for increased numbers of doctors and nurses. Recruits may come from countries that can ill afford to lose their own staff. It would be more ethical and sensible to solve the nursing problems from within the UK by making the conditions of service, not only the salaries, more attractive. And the government is not clear about how it intends to control the escalating costs of health. Unless the Chancellor saves money by stopping expensive military adventures, reducing other important domestic projects such as "education, education, education" or raises taxes, the control of costs in the NHS must be achieved either by rationing, as at present, and/or by reducing the demands. Forthright politicians would say, for example, that expensive new drugs to prevent relapses in multiple sclerosis, hip replacements, or the support by nurses for chronic disorders in the community cannot all be provided. Who then chooses the priorities? A government minister, the government agency for reviewing difficult decisions called the National Institute for Clinical Excellence (NICE), the new unified trusts or the specialist doctors arguing for services for their own patients? Who drives the decisions? Those that have the ear of the minister, the most effective lobby groups, or the *Sun* with its latest horror story or medical debacle?

There are imperfect methods of comparing the changes in quality of life and the costs of different treatments. The inequity of healthcare in the USA is well known but their government has started an Agency for Healthcare Research and Quality to measure the quality of healthcare. An example of inequality is so-called "post-code" prescribing where patients may or may not have expensive treatments depending on where they live. Views on the NHS from healthcare experts from abroad have described it as having "inhumane rationing" or, in another view, as an attempt to use scarce resources in a rational, consensual, civilised way. The UK government has new administrative ideas of unproven value such as awarding "star" ratings, creating foundation hospitals and opening privately run diagnostic and treatment centres. Fortunately the Scottish Executive is avoiding these ideas. Administrators are caught between the political demands and conflicting clinical priorities. Life is an endless round of meetings; those with clinicians may be organised regardless of booked clinics, operating schedules, and ward rounds. New terms are created such as "quality assurance" departments and personnel departments are re-badged "human resources".

Bevan famously stated that consultants would agree to work in the new NHS because he had "stuffed their mouths with gold". Most consultants, in my experience, work very hard with much greater concern for professional services than their incomes. Professional knowledge and expertise are changing. Let me illustrate this from one specialty – neurology. In 1948 there were few neurologists, and they were mainly in London. They pontificated on poorly understood and sometimes obscure neurological conditions. The terminology was impressive but the treatment was limited. Fortunately, more accurate diagnosis and better treatments have emerged for conditions such as epilepsy, Parkinson's disease and multiple sclerosis although there are still no cures. Wonderful new methods of seeing the brain with MRI and CT-scanning help in diagnosis. The demands are great but the resources are limited. There are six-month waiting lists for consultations in many centres, while in Europe, where there are many more neurologists, there are none. Neurosurgical techniques are evolving rapidly but their evaluation is difficult and a research study may be outdated before it reports. Teams not individuals often provide care and similar changes are occurring in all the medical specialties. Now consider the demands on the GP who still has to deal with over eighty per cent of all consultations.

But an important development in clinical practice which might help address these issues and deliver improvements, is "evidence-based medicine". The aim is to adopt good practices and abandon ineffective, dangerous, and wasteful ones. Guidelines for treatment are carefully developed in Scotland by a world-leading endeavour, the Scottish Intercollegiate Guidelines Network (SIGN), supported by the Royal Colleges, the Scottish Executive and the NHS. Thousands of publications are judged on the quality of the evidence on defined criteria. It is curious that political decisions are seldom based on the same rigorous approach to evidence. The long-established GOBSAT technique (Grand Old Boys Sitting Around a Table) is preferred. The government talks of providing good local services, which is an excellent idea when it is appropriate. However some services are better provided nationally, such as microbiology reference laboratories and specialist services for rare conditions. The best way of negotiating these complexities is to replace the informal contacts of old with more organised "managed clinical networks." The idea is to provide a framework for care of people with particular conditions. The "clinical networks" in Scotland should link general practices with hospitals for treatment based on the best available evidence. But they are slow to implement. Guess why! Money again.

The Royal Colleges are historic, prestigious institutions. Handsome oil paintings of previous presidents bedeck the walls and the old libraries are musty. They too seek to maintain a place in a changing medical world. They adapt the post-graduate examinations, courses and lectures that they have run for centuries and advise on medical issues. The General Medical Council is adapting more quickly. It has changed undergraduate medical education greatly in the last decade, encouraging communication skills and ethical attitudes alongside professional competence. It has recommended training for young doctors, registers doctors, including those from abroad, and promotes performance procedures for assessing competence and knowledge of doctors. After criticism, it has altered how it supervises the rogue doctors and the grossly incompetent in their fitness to practice by having a more broadly representative assessment.

The explosion of new information in medicine makes it difficult for doctors, nurses and others to acquire and maintain knowledge and competence. Organised lectures, seminars and discussions in every hospital to meet widely differing needs are complex to organise. Training should be when and where it is needed and at the right level. New technologies of e-learning may prove to be a powerful tool for this. An important development is a largely Scottish initiative, the idea of International Virtual Medical Schools (IVIMEDS) and International Virtual Nursing (IVNurse). The IVIMEDS project, still at an early stage, is starting with undergraduate medical education involving forty medical schools from around the world. This exciting project is being driven by the University of Dundee and in particular Professor Ronald Harden, former Professor of Medical Education at Dundee and the University's Chancellor and Vice-Principal, Sir Alan Langlands. The methods being developed could be widely applicable across the health services.

Medical research is international and much comes from the USA. In the UK, the Medical Research Council can only fund a proportion of the highest rating basic and applied research.

Research in universities is funded from competitive grants. Research teams replace the era of an Alexander Fleming doing isolated pioneering work on his own. while seeking the next research grant, publication of papers and attendance at national or international meetings. The results are unpredictable; while an audit of practical outcomes can be evaluated most rapidly, research into healthcare systems takes longer, and basic research into biomedical aspects of disease such as genetics may or may not provide amazing results in the long term.

Pharmaceutical companies provide mixed benefits for the sick. The drug budget in the NHS is spiralling upward and the profits are high. Some companies have been forced to reduce the exorbitant costs of drugs for AIDS. Some companies target conditions that may yield profit while neglecting research into treatments for rarer conditions and disorders common in developing countries for which the market is limited. However, the companies invest millions in the development of new treatments; some succeed, many fail. Scotland's medical Nobel laureate, Sir James Black, moved between two major pharmaceutical companies and university laboratories as he made his important discoveries and then started an innovative company. Without the drive and investment in both basic research and clinical trials by the pharmaceutical companies there would be fewer drugs today. The private healthcare services also seek profit. Glossy brochures display the quiet, sophisticated, plush offices and the allure of early appointments and prompt treatment. However, selected patients and conditions do not include the long-term ill or the disadvantaged. Nor is continued staff training provided, nor do they participate in research.

Meanwhile the media's agenda is to sell newspapers, magazines and TV programmes. "Breakthroughs" such as an early report of a drug trial or the optimistic results of experiments with rats (timely publicity may help the pharmaceutical company profile) increase expectations. A new surgical technique, with a real life story, published long before a full evaluation, makes good copy. Even better copy are disasters, some deserving coverage such as the multiple murders by Dr Harold Shipman and the debacle over paediatric cardiac surgery deaths in Bristol Royal Infirmary. But the unsung heroes in the health service, the unrecognised carers and satisfied patients are not good copy.

Patients' voices and their rights were discussed earlier but not their responsibilities or the wider social and cultural issues. The idea of taking responsibility for one's own health and of having no more than one's own fair share has not been promoted. If we smoke, drink and eat to excess, if we wish to have tattoos of previous lovers or a relic of a drunken night out removed, if we have lips or breasts that we wish enlarged or reduced are these the responsibility of the National Health Service? "Fair share" can still be seen in patients that don't want to trouble their doctors or to take up too much time when the waiting room is full. It has gone, however, in those that demand immediate visits for trivial non-urgent complaints or otherwise abuse the service. Prevention of illness and injury from drugs, perhaps in a deprived area, requires education, employment opportunities, social support and the law. If children fed on junk food become ill in the future this is partly an educational problem and a marketing issue.

The "welfare of the sick" has had a turbulent course since 1948, with ups and downs. The downs have come from politicians, administrators and some medical professionals who are slow to change. The ups have been from great scientific and technical advances, some of which have come from pharmaceutical companies, and the professionally-driven requirements for evidence for treatment, for clinical networks, for staff to have continued education, and for the skills and knowledge to be more formally assessed. If the ups predominate, then the National Health Service will evolve and can be trusted.

Part II

The Way We See Ourselves

Journalism
Broadcasting

Part II: The Way We See Ourselves

Journalism

Harry Reid

A cynical (American) definition of the newspaper editor: someone who is paid to separate the wheat from the chaff, and then print the chaff. When I started in Scottish journalism in 1969, there was much less chaff in our newspapers, partly because they were thinner than they are now. Papers have not only become bigger; they have become cleaner, brighter and altogether better looking. Design has improved to the extent that design values are sometimes regarded as more important than the actual text.

There are more columnists, analysts and pundits now, but far fewer staff reporters. News may still be king, but only just. And "news" stories, even in the serious papers, are often trivial and personality-driven. There is less deference, which is good, and much more froth, which is bad. There is less deeply researched investigative journalism, and this, alas, is particularly true in Scotland. Features take up far more space.

Speeches made at venerable institutions such as the Houses of Parliament or the General Assembly of the Church of Scotland tended, in the 1960s, to be printed accurately and at great length. Now flimsy extracts are deemed sufficient and sketch writers, as opposed to reporters, are ubiquitous.

Newspapers are not just fatter now; they are often multi-sectioned. There is much more choice for the newspaper-buying public, especially on Sundays.

It is now rare for production to be stopped because of industrial disputes. In the 1960s, 1970s and early 1980s stoppages were all too common. The production chain was complicated and several unions, some of them with very few workers actually engaged in the process, had the power to shut down papers, sometimes for weeks at a time. New computerised technology has brought many benefits, but the standard of text editing has declined.

I don't know if people were conscious that they possessed, or aspired to, "lifestyles" in the 1960s, but readers are not allowed to forget the importance of lifestyle now. Today's papers are perhaps less dull; they are softer, more personality-driven, more frivolous.

In the 1960s business pages tended to be safe and predictable; flamboyance was left to the sportswriters. Newspapers took little interest in television. Again, in the 1960s women journalists were comparatively rare. Marketing men and women were not often seen in newspaper offices, and lawyers were not often consulted by editors. Casual journalists rarely worked in newsrooms. Now papers are routinely put together by casual staff.

In the twenty-first century, focus groups and research surveys are employed to advise editors (who used to operate on a heady mixture of flair, instinct and experience) about what their readers allegedly want. Yet these readers are nothing like so abundant as they once were. And respect for journalists, never high, has declined along with circulation. Two senior but very different British journalists, Lord Hurd and Robin Cook, drew loud and sustained applause at a recent conference in Cheltenham when they attacked contemporary standards in the British press. It is possible that the unthinkable has happened; journalists are even less popular than politicians. Yet vast numbers of intelligent school-leavers want to be journalists, and many universities have schools of journalism.

There are many paradoxes in all this, and it is still far too soon to attempt an obituary of the British newspaper; but the mid-term omens are not good.

After I left university I spent nearly a year at the Thomson Training School in Newcastle, then recently established, learning the basics of reporting. When I arrived at the *Scotsman* in 1969 the paper had only four women working in its august Edinburgh editorial offices. Three of them worked for the near-ghetto of the so-called women's page, the other was a features sub. (One of the quartet, Julie Davidson, was to become my wife.) The best writing on the paper was at the back, where the great John Rafferty (who had succeeded the equally great Hugh McIlvanney, though Hugh was the younger man) was covering football and Norman Mair was writing about golf and rugby.

There were only two columnists. The reporters went out and mixed with their contacts and other reporters and they were for the most part raffish and hard-drinking. The news sub-editors on the back shift were a dour but sedulous group of men (I re-emphasise: no women) who were middle-aged to elderly, wore cardigans and drank bad coffee out of battered flasks. Most of them had vast and eclectic knowledge. They worked with a careful, even pedantic, precision. There was little sense of glamour or excitement. The paper that these people produced was solid, rigorous by today's standards, and disliked and admired by its readers in equal measure. Its sale was rising steadily but slowly. There was little volatility among the paper's staff, or in the paper's sales. The pace was gentle and the tone was earnest. But I soon sensed, as a tyro reporter and sportswriter, that the paper had a purpose, an over-riding sense of direction. And I was right. About two years before I arrived, it had committed to devolution, an almost revolutionary concept at that time. From the late 1960s and through the 1970s, the paper campaigned vigorously for a Scottish Assembly. The intellectual charge was led by the late Professor John Mackintosh, whose Monday column was without doubt the most cerebrally impressive I have ever come across in Scottish journalism.

The *Scotsman* eventually became far too obsessed with its great cause, and in 1979, when the first devolution proposals failed, the paper immediately lost momentum and many of its best journalists quickly departed.

One of the benefits of a Scottish Parliament was supposedly its ability to unite Scotland, to end the age-old and debilitating rivalries between the country's four proud city-states, Aberdeen, Dundee, Edinburgh and Glasgow. Their fierce, independent strengths somehow represented Scotland's collective weakness, its chronic divisiveness. Ironically, one of the most obvious manifestations of these city-states was the quartet of broadsheet newspapers, each one solidly rooted in its own city: respectively the *Press and Journal*, the *Courier*, the *Scotsman* and the *Glasgow Herald*. A prime function of each of these papers was and is to provide thorough and responsible coverage of local news. The *P and J* and the *Courier* fulfilled this function superbly; the *Scotsman* and the *Herald* a little less so. But that is because the latter two are also pan-Scotland, national papers, available thoughout the country. They provide an all-Scotland agenda, and seek, or should seek, to treat Scottish affairs with the dignity and seriousness you would expect from a genuine national press. (This was why the *Glasgow Herald*, in the early 1990s, became the *Herald*; at one point it was going to be the *Scottish Herald*.)

In addition, despite limited resources, the *Scotsman* and the *Herald* aspire to intelligent coverage of British, European and indeed global affairs. They don't always succeed, but they do try valiantly, and at times both papers compare well with their London-based counterparts.

All four papers, but particularly the *Scotsman* and the *Herald*, might have been expected to benefit from the arrival of Scotland's new Parliament in 1999, but it did not work out that way. The *Scotsman*, whose dream this had once been, was by now ambivalent, not to say confused and suspicious, about devolution. The *Herald*, on the other hand, had belatedly picked up the devo-enthusiasm of the *Scotsman*. The *Herald* was also sympathetic to the SNP (the only major paper to be fair to the party, in fact) and this did not go down well with New Labour, whose sinister and thuggish bullying tactics against the paper are graphically recounted by the *Herald*'s Scottish political editor Murray Ritchie in his excellent book, *Scotland Reclaimed* (2000).

If you compare the circulation figures from the autumn of 1999 with those of the autumn of 2003, you will see that the coming of the Parliament has not given the indigenous Scottish press a boost. The *Scotsman*'s sale in late 1999 was 77,000; in 2003, 70,000. The *Herald*'s in 1999 was 106,000; in 2003, 86,000. These figures mask considerable volatility, however. In 2000 the *Scotsman*'s publisher, the abrasive and aggressive Andrew Neil, launched a spectacular price-cutting campaign, slashing the *Scotsman*'s cover price from 45p to 20p. This was combined with an assault on Glasgow.

Although the *Scotsman* was now selling at less than half the price of the *Herald*, the Glasgow paper refused to be drawn into a price war and stood firm. For a time the *Scotsman*'s sales actually overtook those of the *Herald* but they soon declined again as the price campaign could not be sustained, and the breakthrough in Glasgow could not be accomplished. In the last year or so the *Herald*'s circulation has stabilised while that of the *Scotsman* has continued its slow decline. The old pattern of city-state papers resumed and, as the figures show, the *Herald* is currently well ahead of the *Scotsman*.

The king of the broadsheets, however, is the *P and J*, which is currently selling 92,500. Its redoubtable, long-serving editor, Derek Tucker, currently chairman of the Scottish editors' committee, is convinced that the paper's resilience is firmly founded on its concentration on rigorous local news coverage (the paper has seven editions). Surveying the declining market, Tucker says laconically: "We're the healthiest patient in the cancer ward."

The problem patient remains the *Scotsman*. Since Andrew Neil became its publisher at the end of 1996, there have been six editors. Six editors in seven years is not a prescription for stability. The paper reached its nadir in terms of what should be its staple, its news coverage, during the editorship of Rebecca Hardy, a young English woman recruited from the *Daily Mail*, whose news judgment was eccentric, to put it mildly. Luckily, Iain Martin, Hardy's successor, is being given one of an editor's most precious commodities, time, and the paper is gradually recovering its lost authority. The *Herald*'s problem, on the other hand, has not been a quickfire succession of editors (there have been only four in the past 20 years) but changes of ownership; there have been four different owners in the past 10 years. This again is not a prescription for stability but the *Herald* has stuck to its core values and has survived remarkably well.

I mentioned that the *Herald* and the *Scotsman* were genuine pan–Scotland papers, aspiring to national status. This is also of course true of Scotland's pre-eminent tabloid, the *Record*, which has had a wretched time recently. Not so long ago its circulation was 750,000; in the autumn of 1999, soon after the election of the

Scottish Parliament, its sale was 650,000. Now it is down to 515,000. This decline is catastrophic; the main problem has been that the *Record* has simply not known how to counter the energy and cheek of Rupert Murdoch's *Scottish Sun*. In 1998 and 1999 the *Record*'s editor was Martin Clarke, an Englishman who treated Scotland's new Parliament with visceral contempt. The paper he edited was edgy and frenetic and lacked any consistency. His successor Peter Cox was at first more thoughtful but he became bogged down in silly campaigns, and for some reason he took on Celtic Football Club (whose fans, in my experience, are more determinedly loyal than those of Rangers). Cox was also given a bad deal, because Trinity Mirror, the *Record*'s owners, persisted in promoting the *Scottish Mirror* with price-cutting campaigns. How this was supposed to help to sustain the *Record* in an already desperately difficult tabloid market is beyond me. Anyway, earlier this year, the inevitable happened: Cox left and the editor of the *Scottish Sun*, Bruce Waddell, was appointed in his place.

Several Scottish papers have come and gone in the last twenty years; notably the *Sunday Standard*, launched by the *Herald*'s then owners, Lonrho, in 1981, under the dynamic editorship of the legendary Charlie Wilson, who went on to edit the *Times*. The *Standard* was launched at a bad time, one of recession, and it was plagued by commercial problems during its short life. But it was an editorial success, and there was much lamenting when it was shut down in the summer of 1983. The decision came when it was clear that its big sister, the *Herald*, could sustain it no longer. Another paper that has come and gone was *Business AM*. Launched in Edinburgh in 2000 by the Bonnier Group, it was a niche tabloid aimed at Scotland's business community. It employed a remarkable total of seventy-three journalists, and although it was gutsy and lively, its failure to achieve even its own very modest circulation targets ensured its demise.

But the picture is not all gloom and doom. In 1988 the *Scotsman* stable launched *Scotland on Sunday*, which rapidly established itself as an intelligent all-Scotland title. The *Sunday Times* responded with an ambitious revamp of its Scottish edition, and in 1999 the Scottish Media Group, then owners of the *Herald*, launched the *Sunday Herald* in Glasgow.

Like *Scotland on Sunday*, the *Sunday Herald* rapidly developed its own distinctive tone and a useful editorial mix. Both papers have managed to establish loyal readerships in a desperately crowded market. *SOS* is currently selling 85,000 per Sunday, the *Sunday Herald* 61,000.

The other significant positive in the Scottish press scene at the moment is the resilience of the local weekly and bi-weekly sector.

One truth should be clear from all this: Scots newspaper consumers have plenty of choice. They have always been able to purchase London-based titles if that was their wont; and since the early 1990s, after Rupert Murdoch slashed the price of the *Times* and an all-out price war ensued, London papers have seen Scotland, not so much as a soft market, but a wide-open one. We have grown used to "Scottish editions" of London-based titles. The Scottish news may be largely spurious, but these papers have vast resources, and they deploy every trick in the marketing book. Thus the Scottish newspaper market is now routinely described as the most competitive in Europe. I am sceptical about this (how comparisons with say Greece or Finland or Lithuania are measured, I don't know) but there can be no doubt that the Scottish market is characterised by a feverish intensity that was undreamed of thirty-five years ago.

Competitive markets encourage marketeers, and that is not necessarily a blessing for newspaper executives. I was always suspicious of one of the great marketing mantras, the need to attract younger and younger readers. Papers which have overtly tried to woo younger readers have often seen larger circulation falls than their more stately peers. I used to tell marketing people about the grannies in the Russian churches. People used to point out that the churches were filled with grannies; no young folk. Thus the Church would die. Yet, there somehow turned out to be a constant supply of new grannies.

I don't wish to be complacent, but we should also remember that the over–fifties have huge spending power (they account for more than forty per cent of consumer demand) and they are a growing segment of the population. They also use the internet more than any other group: and online papers remain a serious if undeveloped threat to traditional papers printed on newsprint. Finally, older writers can write with a zest and a freshness that can put their younger colleagues to shame: Ron Ferguson, in the *Press and Journal* and in the *Herald*, is a case in point.

To conclude with some unashamedly personal comments and prejudices. What saddens me most about the Scottish press is the decline of good sportswriting. I have had the enormous privilege of working with the late John Rafferty, Norman Mair, the late Ian Archer, and Doug Gillon (thankfully Doug is still writing well). I see talent in the likes of Graham Spiers and Jim Traynor but they have not yet found that elusive talisman: authority. Indeed I reckon the distinguished football writer Glenn Gibbons, in the *Scotsman*, writes with an easy magistracy that his much younger colleagues cannot yet find.

Despite the growing tendency to tabloidise (please forgive the ugly word) which is partly a function of our chronic transport system, with its overcrowded buses, trains and even planes, I still like the broadsheet format. I was delighted, just the other day, to see the *Herald* launching its new ABC (Arts Books and Cinema) section as a broadsheet. This will showcase some of its best writers, such as Rosemary Goring, Michael Tumelty and Hannah McGill (Hannah McGill, incidentally, was a winner in the *Herald*'s student journalism awards, an excellent project to encourage good journalism by students). I think broadsheets let writing breathe as tabloids never can.

I'd like to see more investigative journalism. This kind of reporting is expensive and risky; you can have a couple of reporters digging for a month, and then the story won't stand up, or the lawyers will insist that it is far too dangerous to publish. But there are still some dogged, digging journalists around. The *Herald*'s Simon Bain was Scottish Journalist of the Year in 2000 for his exposure of petrol price fixing in the Highlands, a thrawn and brave investigation that took on multi-national interests of great power. I'd love to see more of this kind of work.

I have been pleased to note the developing excellence of the business/economics sector in the UK press. People like Patience

Wheatcroft and Anatole Kaletsky in the *Times* are writing superbly. In Scotland, Bill Jamieson in the *Scotsman* writes well, but the champion in this area remains the superlative Alf Young, whose columns in the *Herald* and *Sunday Herald* are required reading for anyone who is concerned about the condition of Scotland.

I enjoy reading readers' letters (some journalists take a petty and condescending view of letters pages, believing that only professional writers can write succinctly and pertinently. Day in, day out, our letter writers prove them wrong). The best letters page, I believe, remains that of the *Herald*, edited by the veteran Andrew Hood, who was doing the job for the *Scotsman* (among other things) forty years ago. The *Herald*'s letters seem to me a fascinating forum that comes close to what the playwright Arthur Miller said a newspaper should be all about, a nation talking to itself. To be fair, the *Scotsman*'s letters have been improving lately.

If I could change one thing, it would be to give editors and other senior journalists a little thinking time. To produce a brand new product, day in, day out, is heady and exciting; few other people have this privilege in their quotidian working lives. Yet this very short-term stimulation militates against the longer view. For most editors, strategic thinking means the middle of next week. Newspaper owners should encourage their editors to take sabbaticals, to read more than other newspapers, to think more and ponder more. Of course, this is all very well, but the industry is consumed with paranoia and presenteeism; if you are away for six weeks, who will be sitting in your chair when you return?

More than anything, our Scottish press needs to calm down, to have the confidence to reject the modish and the meretricious, and to recover the virtues of reflection and thoughtfulness. Above all, it needs to rediscover the merits of simple news-gathering.

Part II: The Way We See Ourselves

Broadcasting

Magnus Linklater

Ten years ago I contributed a review of Scottish broadcasting for a book called *Anatomy of Scotland*. It was a fairly chirpy, upbeat account of television and radio production, which made the point that audiences north of the border were reasonably well served with a mixture of home-grown and UK output. They demonstrated a keen appetite for Scottish programmes, but were unwilling to be fobbed off with anything that dropped below the UK standard. There were some familiar complaints from the broadcasters themselves, about under-funding, cut-backs in jobs, and resentment at London arrogance, but by and large the mood was optimistic. "We are the voice of the nation," announced Pat Chalmers, the then controller of BBC Scotland. "The nation wants its own agenda," said Gus Macdonald, the managing director of Scottish Television, "It is more important than ever to have one that is identifiably Scottish."

Both could point to some impressive achievements. Scottish Television was promising 340 extra hours of broadcasting in Scotland. BBC Scotland had just produced the network production *Tutti Frutti* by John Byrne, with its successor, *Your Cheatin' Heart*, and an adaptation of Melvyn Bragg's *A Time to Dance*. There were plays by Tom Kempinski, Alan Plater, William McIlvanney, Trevor Griffiths and David Mamet. The then head of BBC's television drama department, Bill Bryden, had staged a massive production called *The Ship*, set in Clydeside, and filmed in its entirety by BBC's music and arts department. Judith Weir's new work for Scottish Opera, *The Vanishing Bridegroom*, had been produced on television, and *Rab C. Nesbitt* had proved so successful that it had been taken over by BBC 2. It was Chalmers' boast that the £15 million spent by the BBC on arts projects in Scotland made them a greater patron than the Scottish Arts Council.

It seemed inevitable that devolution would unleash more of the same. While broadcasting remained a reserved matter, still under supervision from Westminster, the new political era suggested that there would be a growing appetite for strong local programming. With talented journalists, documentary-makers and playwrights waiting in the wings, there seemed no reason to doubt that the advent of a new parliament would accompany a cultural resurgence on radio and television. When Kirsty Wark, presenter of the BBC's flagship political programme, *Left, Right and Centre*, took the platform at the Usher Hall in early 1992, in front of a 2,500-strong audience, to host the *Scotsman* debate on devolution, she appeared to many to represent the power and the promise of the Scottish media.

To say that what has transpired is a disappointment would be to miss the point. Devolution has not turned out the way we expected, so why should broadcasting? Since the Parliament, which was intended to meet the wishes of the Scottish people, has been something of an anti-climax thus far, it is hardly surprising to record that there has been equally little evidence of a new climate in Scottish broadcasting. BBC Scotland's most recent annual report is a curious mixture of bravado and uncertainty. It lays great stress on connecting with its audience, highlights programmes which deal with day-to-day life, and is defensive on its decision to plough much of its resources into establishing a Scottish television soap opera, *River City*.

In assessing its progress against objectives, it emphasises, first, sports coverage, second events, such as the Hogmanay Festival in Edinburgh, then semi-documentary programmes such as a series on Ninewells Hospital, another hospital series, *Baby ER*, set in a maternity hospital in Glasgow, *Raploch Stories* about life on a housing scheme on the outskirts of Stirling, *Lives Less Ordinary* about ordinary people caught up in extraordinary circumstances, and *Tales from the Edge,* also about life on the margins of society. Comedy comes next, *The Karen Dunbar Show,* various spin-offs from the comedy series *Chewin' the Fat*, and a football comedy road-show, *Offside*. It is curiously hesitant about endorsing *River City*, saying only that it is "monitoring its performance". It pays tributes to its news and current affairs programmes, and promises more research.

It concedes that drama is weak; indeed, it is safer to say there is none. Under the heading, it simply mentions *River City*. There are semi-documentaries like *A Thousand Acres of Sky*, and programmes in the *Ex-S* series, with titles like *Scotland's Best Chippie*, *Hen Nights* and *Miracle Child*. There was a good documentary series about the Scottish regiments, called *The Real Tartan Army*, but the sole gesture towards the arts is the *Artworks* programme which is, however, intermittent. The BBC still commissions short eight or ten-minute films called *Tartan Shorts*. But there is no mention any more of feature-length films such as the much-trumpeted *Mrs Brown*, starring Billy Connolly. One thing has not changed. Back in 1992 there was a pawky Scots sit-com called *Strathblair*. Today there is a pawky Scots sit-com called *Monarch of the Glen*. We can't quite seem to get it out of our system. I do not want to be too unfair. Much of this down-market trend reflects the general development of television in Britain. It would be hard, however, to conclude from this that there had been a genuine burst of distinctive, original and creative Scottish programming.

Over on Scottish Television and Grampian, there is a similar sense of diminution. Regional output has shrunk considerably, from 800 hours to 626, though more people, it seems, tune into those Scottish programmes which are on offer. I was amazed, on tuning into their web-site, to see that, under the heading of drama, Scottish Television itself listed as "your favourite programmes": *Dr Findlay*, *The Pride* [sic] *of Miss Jean Brodie*, *Taggart* and *Take the High Road*, though the latter, after 21 years, is not going back into production. Whether this kailyard diet is a serious reflection of the new era in Scotland is, as they say, for others to judge. A documentary series called *This Scotland* is running, but on the week I looked, the principal offering was a programme called *The One Button Suit* about naturism in Scotland. There is a single arts programme on Scottish called *Artery*, and one on Grampian called *Off the Wall.* It is, however, worth noting that Scottish and Grampian do seem to have made an effort to tap into the potential amongst young film-makers. *Newfoundland* is a series which commissions young Scottish directors to make a series of half- hour films, and they have done eighteen so far, using leading Scottish actors like Ewan McGregor, Peter Mullen, Pam Ferris, Billy Boyd and David Hayman. Two of their films, *Afterlife* and *Blinded*, produced in 2003, were seen at the Edinburgh Film Festival.

So what happened to the great debate about Scottish broadcasting? Because the Scottish Parliament has no remit here, broadcasting being a reserved matter, there has been no committee inquiry north of the border, though there have been debates on the floor of the house. The Scottish Select Committee at Westminster did hold hearings a couple of year ago, when the main topics of discussion centred round the "Scottish Six" and the *Newsnight* opt-out. These are two perennial topics for anyone who takes an interest in how a devolved Scotland deals with news and current affairs. It had always been an article of faith amongst pro-devolutionists that as soon as Scotland had established its parliament it would also have a Scottish six o'clock news. Both BBC and ITV fenced around the issue, but decided eventually to postpone a decision. Today, that decision remains postponed. There has, however, been a controversial opt-out, nightly, on BBC-2, whereby *Newsnight*, introduced in London by Jeremy Paxman or Kirsty Wark, splits off at 11pm into a special Scottish version.

Everyone has a view on whether it works or not. Paxman himself was outraged that his programme was being truncated, and, for the viewer, it is often infuriating, when a key subject, like the Middle East, is being debated, to be switched suddenly through to a discussion on exam league tables in Scotland or whether there is a future for the Scottish fishing industry. It smacks of tokenism, of compromise, and more than a streak of condescension. Having said that, it is professionally done, and viewing figures are said to be surprisingly good. The Scottish Six issue has been raised again, and a major review is being carried out by the BBC to assess its viewers' attitude to the idea, as well as other changes to news and current affairs. So far, figures suggest that the current news hour on BBC-1 between 6pm and 7pm performs well in Scotland, with both the *Six O'clock News* and *Reporting Scotland* well ahead of ITV. One proposition being tested is that television news could be integrated, so that BBC Scotland produced and presented a single programme encompassing international, UK and Scottish news. Demonstration tapes have been made of how such a programme might work, and are being tested out on viewers. The timetable for the review envisages that BBC Scotland will have reached conclusions by the end of 2003.

I have not seen the tapes, and know nothing of whether the idea would work. But I doubt if it would be an improvement. To ensure that an hour-long Scottish-produced news programme would be up to the standard of the UK version, there would have to be considerably greater funding than is currently available, and nothing about *Reporting Scotland* suggests that there is either the range of subject-matter or the resources to raise its game in the way that viewers would demand. If, over the past three years, BBC Scotland had demonstrated a genuine drive to improve its Scottish current affairs programmes, it might be able to argue that there was not only the demand for more, but the talent and the enthusiasm to produce it. A proposal that there should be a serious, early evening discussion programme has been abandoned, presumably through lack of interest. A Scottish Six programme should emerge only because it is needed, not because it simply sounds the right thing to do. So far that need has not been demonstrated.

My principal complaint about post-devolution broadcasting centres, however, on radio. What on earth has happened to Radio Scotland? Why is it that Scottish listeners are now treated to a down-market radio station with a bare minimum of serious programming, while Radio Four, its equivalent station in London, has gone in precisely the opposite direction? Why is it that we are assumed to be capable only of listening to jaunty comedy shows, sport, or phone-ins? Is there no intellectual life in Scotland any more? Is there no appetite for serious debate or discussion? Is there nothing of interest going on in this country? Back in 1992, I was able to review a range of programmes, such as drama, documentaries, music and discussion, which had won several international awards. Today those pretensions have been almost wholly abandoned, and the listener to Radio Scotland will search in vain for searching, challenging, or in-depth programmes of any serious consequence.

Of course there are exceptions. I except *Good Morning Scotland*, which remains essential listening, and which is as professional as anything to be heard south of the border. I except *News Drive* and the one, hour-long *Arts Show*, which hangs on there in the early evening. I except Edi Stark who is intelligent and incisive. I am dismayed, however, that the *Eye to Eye* programme on Sunday, which used to be presented by Ruth Wishart, is no longer to be heard. What dismays me most, however, is the one-dimensional nature of this station, the relentless cheeriness of it, the sameness of its daily programming, the lack of anything at all to get your teeth into. A glance through its schedules reveals what I mean.

Fred Macaulay is, of course, the nation's favourite comedian. Thus he is on, every morning, jaunty and jolly, from nine to ten. His subjects range (I quote at random) from talking seals to the talents of Lionel Blair, from model car racing to boxing housewives. It is all good fun, of course, and it is there, without exception, daily. Then there is Gary Robertson, a workmanlike presenter, who deals in workmanlike subjects. I have listened quite often to his discussions on street crime, on hospital waiting lists, on motor-cycling, on zoos, on the mounting piles of disposable nappies: you name it, Gary will talk about it. I hope he will not mind, however, if I observe that there is a certain sameness about his style. His conclusions are rarely earth-shattering, his guests are drawn from that range of experts one can only categorise as "the usual suspects". It is, in short, worthy. And again it is there, every day, for an hour and a half.

And then there is two hours of Lesley Riddoch. Combative, feisty, opinionated, you either love her or you hate her. But there is no avoiding her. She stands for opinion in Scotland today, and we have, I suppose, to accept that. It is, however, an opinion that is set in Lesley's particular brand of concrete. On all the key issues – public spending, the economy, health and education, the arts, land reform and so on – Lesley's views are by now well-known. She doesn't like "the establishment", she finds Tories risible, she refers to people with land or money as "toffs", she is against public schools, she is for the workers and against the bosses, she is still fighting the class war, with all her prejudices triumphantly on display. And since this is a phone-in programme, her listeners respond likewise. There is, I suppose, nothing wrong with this, and I dare say Radio Scotland has the listening figures to justify these two prime-time hours given over to Lesley five days a week. It does not, however, allow for much rational, informed discussion. By contrast, Radio Four's morning programming has majored on it.

The contrast could not be starker. From Monday to Friday, the gamut is run from *Start the Week*, a cultural discussion programme with Andrew Marr, to *Book of the Week*, which, on the week I listened, was a serialisation of Redmond O'Hanlon's account of trawling, mostly in Scottish waters. I heard a programme on Brazil's first black woman senator, a profile of Dorothy Hodgkin, the Nobel-prize-winning scientist, a discussion on sensation in the Victorian novel, an account of Scotland's nineteenth century answer to Darwin, an investigation into Erskine Childers' *Riddle of the Sands*, the excellent *Moral Maze*, debating moral issues of the day, and a series on migration. Then, in the afternoon, there was drama, and there was reading.

Radio Scotland no longer does drama, or much reading. And so we hear nothing of the current crop of Scottish writers, though everyone knows that we are undergoing something of a literary renaissance. No Liz Lochhead, no Ian Rankin, no William McIlvanney, no A. L. Kennedy, no Alan Warner, no David Greig, no James Kelman, no Alasdair Gray, no Allan Massie, no Iain Banks, no Douglas Dunn, no Alan Spence. How long have we got? There used to be a programme called *Storyline,* fifty minutes of reading with a Scottish bias, five days a week. It has gone. Yet these writers and others do get an airing. There are plays and readings being commissioned – and commissioned in Scotland. Bizarrely, a team employed by Radio Scotland produces more than sixty hours of plays and readings a year, many of them from Scottish writers or with Scottish themes. And where do they appear? On Radio Four or

Radio Three. About a tenth of Radio Four's drama and reading programmes come from Scotland. They are there thanks to a thing called MOGs, Minimum Output Guarantees. The commissioning costs are paid for by Radio Four or Three, but the ideas, and the creative input, comes from Scotland. Over the past year, there have been dramatisations of *Adam Bede*, *Sherlock Holmes*, *Anna Karenina*, *The Mill on the Floss*, *The Prime of Miss Jean Brodie*, plays by David Greig, Andrew Dallmeyer, and Stewart Conn, readings by James Robertson, Ian Heggie and Liz Lochhead. None of this, however, is for Scottish consumption, unless, of course, you tune into Radio Four. So what is the explanation for this cultural divide?

The most surprising view I have heard came from a senior figure in BBC Scotland, who said that the station was not pretending to offer as broad an agenda as Radio Four. Instead, if listeners liked "that kind of thing", they could tune in to Radio Four or Three, or pick up on Radio Five. By "that kind of thing" he meant, presumably, culture. What this suggests is that the discerning listener, who is looking for intelligent discussion, who wants more arts and culture, who wants, in short, the stimulation of original ideas, has to tune in to a London-based station. This is, frankly, a scandal. They are being told in effect that the BBC in Scotland no longer caters for the intelligent middle class – that there is, in effect, no intellectual class left in Scotland, or, if there is, then it has to seek its interest and stimulation elsewhere. The nation that produced Lord Reith has reversed his dictum and narrowed rather than widened the choice open to its audience.

It may be that the notion of nation speaking to nation no longer applies. And it is true that I have not heard the phrase "voice of the nation", once used so passionately, issuing recently from Queen Margaret Drive. But if it did, then I suspect that bodies would be revolving in their subterranean graves, and we would hear the sound of hollow, Reithian laughter.

Part III

The Way We Live

Race
Sectarianism
Mental Health

Part III: The Way We Live

Race

Rowena Arshad

I write this from the perspective of someone whose work is in the area of promoting race equality in Scotland. However, I am also a parent with two teenagers who both consider themselves to be Scottish and mixed race. Their father is a white Scot. So I have a vested interest in wishing to see a Scotland that is inclusive, accepting and comfortable with difference and diversity. Allan Massie writing in the *Scotsman* in October 2003 optimistically suggests that in Scotland, we are slowly leaving racism behind. For him, anti-racist discourse is winning. Like me, he reflects upon this as a parent. He sees in his children a growing confidence of living and being in a society that is culturally and ethnically diverse. They are enlightened and hopefully able to live in the world dreamt of by Robert Burns in which "man to man the world o'er, shall brothers be, for a'that" (or should that be, in these politically correct times, people to people the world o'er...).

I would suggest that it has been the influence of different music styles which has done a lot to reshape youth perceptions of race issues. When Eminem, a white working-class boy, started doing rap and becoming associated with black people like Tupac Shakur and Snoopdogg (fellow rap artistes), it began to influence how white working-class young men related to a range of issues, including their associations with blacks. His music created a synthesis between black street culture and white youth so bridging the cultural gap between the two. This in turn leads to greater understanding and acceptance of the "other". The use of Asian bhangra music in television adverts has begun to popularise both Asian culture and music, to the extent that Punjabi MC, whose song is associated with promoting a Peugeot car, won them the Best Dance Album during the MTV awards held in Edinburgh in November 2003. So like Massie, I do detect the change he is referring to. Having lived in Scotland for nearly twenty years, there would appear to be a growing acceptance by the spectrum of Scottish citizens of diversity, an awareness of the presence of racism and a need to challenge it where it exists. A ground-breaking survey of Scottish teenagers commissioned by YouthLink Scotland, conducted by Mori and published in October 2003, found that seven out of ten regarded terms such as "Chinky" or "Paki", and speaking negatively in private or public about people from other ethnic backgrounds, as racist.

I came across Allan Massie's article when I decided to conduct a search of Scotland's newspapers in the past year on the topic of "race". There is certainly a lot more written about racism in this decade than there has been in the past. However the search also threw up some surprises for me. I found within local and national papers, a catalogue of small reports about racist incidents and occurrences that I had not previously come across. As someone who works in the field of race equality and therefore has access to a range of race equality networks, I had assumed a fair grasp of race issues, particularly those involving racial incidents or attacks. The research threw up examples of racist incidents against visible minorities as well as occurrences against people because of their ethnicity or association with some historical event, such as attacks against Germans, South African whites, white English people or people who looked like "terrorists"!

While none of these variations of racism are new to me, what it did reveal was how easy it would be to remain oblivious to racism if it does not affect you or someone you know. Yet, a slight probe of the papers confirms that there remains a shocking level of racist crime in Scotland. During the period April 2001 to March 2002, Strathclyde Police recorded 1,495 racist incidents, an increase of twenty-five per cent on the previous year. While this might be attributed to events post September 11 as well as better reporting mechanisms, what cannot be denied is that these incidents took place. The report also stated that asylum seekers were more vulnerable to crimes of violence than other complainers of racist incidents. What is more worrying is that the theory of the enlightened next generation that I have referred to earlier appears to fall apart as the report concludes that the majority of offenders were white males under the age of thirty. The YouthLink survey mentioned earlier also found that a worryingly high number of youngsters were reporting that they had been a victim of abuse as a result of their race or ethnic group. YouthLink suggests that some of these could also be about anti-English attitudes as well as race/sectarian abuse.

But racism is more than just racist incidents, the absence of which would signal all was well. Racial harmony is no indicator of racial justice. While crude racism is probably now being addressed – for example very few people would wish to be associated with the likes of the racist police recruits exposed in the now infamous documentary *The Secret Policeman* (BBC October 2003) – this form of racism is probably the easiest to identify and tackle. It is the subtle forms of racism which are more worrying.

During the Edinburgh International Festival, I attended *Strictly Dandia,* a performance by a group of young Asian actors and dancers from the Tamasha Theatre Company in London aspiring to be the Indian equivalent of *Strictly Ballroom.* The scene is set during the time of Navratri, the nine nights of dancing leading up to the Hindu festival of lights. At the end of the performance, a woman sitting behind me muttered rather loudly that she would not have attended the performance if she had realised this was a cast of all Asians. As we exited the hall, this person's opinions about "difficulty in understanding their accents" kept on coming. This was not said for my benefit, although I was just behind her. She was rather oblivious, I suspect, of my presence. I wonder if she would have been as vocal if she had noticed me? The racism of this woman involved no violence or the use of racial slurs nor was there an intended victim as such. However, this brand of racism typifies an underlying set of attitudes towards people who are not like us, that is still all too prevalent in Scotland. On that occasion, my fellow theatre-goer seemed to me to be expressing her own personal difficulty with understanding and coming to terms with the extent of the racial, cultural and linguistic diversity that makes up modern-day Britain.

While attitudes like this are as likely to be caused by ignorance as anything else, the entire matter of race and immigration has had an extensive airing and some very heated public debate as a consequence of the mass outcry about the Dungavel Detention Centre. Many people who previously had not seriously considered issues of race will have been exposed to this debate in terms of human rights. Public outrage was fuelled by government determination to maintain the status quo and the failure of Scottish Labour MSPs to comment, far less criticise, the government in Westminster. While there undoubtedly has been an element of the popular pastime of government bashing, the issues that arose will have highlighted for many people that race, nationality or religion can, and do, act as triggers for treatment that has serious human rights implications. It would be unfortunate if the momentum generated by this debate were to be lost. Ideally it should be redirected into wider debate about discrimination and disadvantage as the treatment of asylum seekers can be seen as typifying institutional approaches to discrimination. I would hope that on reflection, government ministers and Scottish Labour MSPs realise that their assumption that the general public are sufficiently ignorant or complacent to support racist immigration and asylum policies was misplaced.

It also seems to me that the war against Iraq earlier this year has once again brought into focus public attitudes about Islam. In the aftermath of 9/11 there was a clear backlash against Muslims, but with significant public opinion against the war, the attitudes at least among the general public might have changed a little. However, in a more global context, I fear it has created a Christian West versus Islamic East divide. Scotland needs to work hard to avoid being in the slipstream of such American-led conflict and ideologies which clearly have racial implications.

On St.Andrew's Day 2002, the Race Relations (Amendment) Act was enacted in Scotland. This legislation places a positive duty on all Scottish public authorities to proactively and explicitly prevent racial discrimination, promote equal opportunities and good relations between people of different ethnic groups. This law was a consequence of the Stephen Lawrence inquiry and the deliberations of Lord Macpherson of Cluny. This public duty makes race-related law one of the most effective of all current UK equality laws. What this law does is to make it compulsory for all public sector bodies to consider the impact of their policies and practice in terms of race, nationality, colour and ethnicity. In the past, public sector bodies had an "ad hoc" attitude to race. The greatest take-up of race equality issues occurred, unsurprisingly, in areas with higher numbers of minority ethnic populations while other areas with lower numbers chose largely to view race matters as irrelevant. This allowed a perpetuation of the myth that racism was an urban issue. Now, all public bodies in Scotland have to consider race equality issues – it is no longer a matter of choice.

While it is early days to gauge how successful this piece of legislation has been, early indications suggest that it is making considerable impact. For a start, public sector managers are having to consider race issues as a significant part of planning, monitoring and evaluation of public services. Combined with the impact of the Disability Discrimination Act, the entire equalities field has been placed firmly on the agenda of public servants as part of their daily work routine. In some cases it would be fair to say that the legislation has provided committed staff with the leverage that they have long needed to overcome institutional resistance, complacency and ignorance and create new scenarios and ideas with which to inform the services that their employers provide to the public. In other cases, the fear of potential litigation has provided the spur to long-overdue action and for some, it has been "a big stick" which they cannot ignore whatever their own beliefs, values or professional inadequacies. At long last, race equality is gaining recognition as an area of required professional expertise, customer care and public duty.

The Scottish Parliament and Scottish Executive have taken the lead on race issues and, to their credit, this leadership came long before the onset of the public duty. The Parliament's Equal Opportunities Committee has worked hard to raise awareness of groups that are often excluded even within the most articulate anti-racist circles, such as gypsy/travellers. The Executive's public awareness campaign, *One Scotland: Many Cultures,* has begun to signal that the governing strata of Scotland does not intend to tolerate racism and is actively trying to create more informed views within the general public. While cynical readers might argue this is publicity politics and others might argue that the title *One Scotland: Many Cultures* dilutes the message of racism and anti-racism, I would assert that doors which were once closed are now open. Being proactive on equality issues is now viewed as good standard practice. Of course there is much more to do in the area of governance and the danger now is that we will become once again complacent, assuming the journey that has been started is complete.

For the first time in Scotland, in 2002 a module of questions was included in the Scottish Social Attitudes (SSA) survey in order to examine the extent and character of discriminatory attitudes in Scotland on disability, gender, sexual orientation and ethnicity. The research was undertaken by NatCen Scotland with the support and collaboration of the Commission for Racial Equality, the Disability Rights Commission, the Equal Opportunities Commission, Stonewall Scotland and the Scottish Executive. This survey suggests that there are two competing visions of Scotland at the beginning of the twenty-first century. The first suggests that Scotland is a socially conservative society, while the second argues that Scotland is an outward-looking, tolerant society. I would argue that this is now a tired record that needs to be discarded. A country, like its people, is likely to be complex and hence can be both, rather than either or. What is more important is that we examine and learn from the data arising from the survey of 1655 people across Scotland in the summer of 2002. From the survey we learn that:

Fifty-six per cent said that there is a great deal of prejudice in Scotland against people from different racial or ethnic backgrounds

Eleven per cent of people said they would prefer a white MSP

Fifty-two per cent of people said that they prefer to live in an area with similar kinds of people to themselves

Eleven per cent of people with a degree said they would mind if a relative married someone from a different racial or ethnic background, compared with twenty-one per cent of those with no qualifications. Similarly, twenty-nine per cent of those aged sixty-five and over took that view compared with six per cent of those aged eighteen to twenty-four years.

What is clear is that there remains work to be done to educate people against racism and prejudice and those at every level committed to race equality and tackling racism need to consider how to reduce the percentages above by the time there is a next attitudes survey.

So, to the future! Having accepted that we need to consider race issues as part of mainstream Scottish thinking, we should deepen our understandings and discussions about the issues. For example, we should no longer accept a black/white dichotomy of the operations of racism. Anti-racists who continue to beat the polarised drum need to mature and consider, indeed take ownership of, the complexities of race and racism as it interweaves with other facets of identity, such as one's gender, sexual orientation, disability, age, social class, faith, secular beliefs and so forth. Racism takes many forms and will shape itself according to the economics, geography and history of the time. Single issue or siloed approaches just will not be appropriate or relevant as people are not one-dimensional.

It would therefore be naive and unhelpful to make the assumption that racism is all one-way traffic. Prejudice is not the sole preserve of white people. Racial prejudices within minority communities also require exposure and discussion. A recent case in Glasgow of a Muslim successfully winning a discrimination case against his Sikh employers bears this out. What is critical here is that anti-racist or anti-discrimination actions and legislation apply equally to all. Demonising white people will only serve to create defensive reactions, which will limit progress and make mutual respect between ethnic groups harder to achieve. An open and honest acknowledgement of responsibility and a commitment to create change can only happen in the context of shared understandings of the nature and history of the divisions and common prejudices that artificially divide us all.

Kenan Malik, a leading academic on race issues in Britain, writing in the the Commission for Racial Equality publication

Connections (Winter 2001), argues that cultural diversity only makes sense within a framework of common values and beliefs that enable us to treat all people equally. To create such a framework requires more dialogue and perhaps a willingness to be less afraid to speak out in case we are accused of racism or intolerance. Malik argues that multi-culturalism has entrenched the divisions created by racism by making cross-cultural interaction more difficult by encouraging people to assert their cultural differences. He said this has allowed people to pursue "parallel lives" which has helped to create divisions and tensions within and between different communities whether that be on grounds of colour, religion, culture or ethnicity.

Malik is not against multi-culturalism as such, if it is contextualised within a general framework that allows all to work together against discrimination and will proactively create bridges. He feels the real failure of multi-culturalism is its failure to understand what is valuable about diversity. To do this, we need to compare and contrast different values, beliefs and lifestyles and decide collectively which to keep and which to change. If we fail to do this then we remain in parallel tracks that will lead us further apart rather than build solidarity and social cohesion.

In a lecture for the Institute of Contemporary Scotland in April 2002, I spoke of the "polite" racism that we in Scotland must now confront. Going back to the very start of this chapter, the woman I met while watching *Strictly Dandia* would probably have been quite pleasant to me but underlying that pleasantness were attitudes which were probably racially prejudiced. Polite racism will ensure inclusion but never equity. Those who are politely racist will engage with the discourse of inclusion where "separate" is tolerated and accepted but never treated as equal. Neil Bissoondatha, a Trinidadian Canadian novelist living in Quebec City, suggests that tolerance is a poor tool for building cohesion in a multi-ethnic society. Post September 11, he saw the façade of multi-culturalism and tolerance in his home country, Canada, crumble as quickly as the World Trade Centre's twin towers. He quotes the late novelist, and fellow Canadian, Robertson Davies who had this to say about tolerance; "Tolerance is a fragile construct built on wilful ignorance. It implies a purposeful turning away from one's neighbour – from the accent, the skin colour, the exotic clothes. It is a shrug of indifference, tinged with condescension. It says: I'll enjoy your curries, admire your costumes, tap my feet to your music; I'll suppress my slight discomfort at the sight of you and your kind in the street, and I will put up with your presence. Don't expect me to truly accept you as one of us, though, especially when the chips are down."

The limits of this chapter prevent me exploring other deep issues such as the interplay between race, racism, territorial tensions in communities and sectarianism. Nor does it allow me to fully interrogate the apparent tolerance of anti-English racism. But on an optimistic final note, I would suggest that we have begun the journey on race matters in Scotland. The 100-metre dash is now complete, we now need to fortify ourselves for the marathon, which will need engagement in honest talking on many of the issues identified above. We have shown as a community and country that we have the capacity and commitment to do this.

Part III: The Way We Live

Sectarianism

Fred Shedden

Some four years have passed since James MacMillan, one of Scotland's leading composers, gave a lecture at the Edinburgh International Festival entitled "Scotland's Shame". Using powerful and emotive language MacMillan spoke of the anti-Catholicism which in his view was rife throughout Scottish society. The reaction to MacMillan's speech was extraordinary. Passionate letters for and against the points made by him dominated the letters pages of the *Herald* and the *Scotsman* for weeks and it seemed that for better or worse the issue of sectarianism in Scotland was at last being openly discussed. Indirectly the controversy was a contributory factor in the formation of Nil by Mouth. Cara Henderson, whose school friend Mark Scott had been murdered in 1995 in a brutal sectarian attack, was much affected by the tone and content of the published letters, many of which seemed to confirm the religious divide in Scotland. After discussion with family and friends Cara vowed to campaign against sectarianism and in August 2000 Nil by Mouth was formally launched. So what has happened in the intervening period?

I was driving home recently listening, as is my wont, to Radio Five Live. I like its mix of sport and news; I enjoy its whimsical and irreverent style. But the report I heard by James Shaw on the aftermath of the first Rangers/Celtic game of the 2003/4 season was neither whimsical nor irreverent. "The Old Firm clash at Ibrox," began Shaw, "passed without major incident, but behind the scenes the emergency services are dealing with the consequences of something like a low-level war between Rangers and Celtic fans."

Reporting from Monklands Hospital's accident and emergency unit, on the border of what he described as "mainly Protestant Airdrie and Coatbridge which is historically Catholic," Shaw went on to catalogue a horrifying list of injuries caused to Rangers and Celtic fans alike by a motley array of weaponry, including a broken bottle, baseball bats and a samurai sword.

What Shaw described was no isolated incident. Unison, many of whose members work in the National Health Service, has reported that on Old Firm match days admissions to accident and emergency units, due to injuries caused by assault, soar in many different parts of Scotland. The number of physical and verbal attacks on NHS staff also rises on the days of these games. One of the saddest features of Shaw's report was his comment that all of this mayhem goes "largely unreported by the media". What kind of society have we become when we appear to tolerate the intolerable? Can you imagine the public outcry and media frenzy which would ensue if this level of violence was occurring on a regular basis between white and Asian youths? Or between Muslims and Hindus? So why are we so apparently blasé about violence between Catholics and Protestants?

Patently football alone is not responsible for all the sectarian ills in our society. The reality is, however, that so-called fans of both Rangers and Celtic continue to commit violent offences which are fuelled by sectarian hatred. The clubs themselves would claim to have taken action in recent years to reduce sectarian behaviour amongst their supporters. Celtic have had their "Bhoys against Bigotry" campaign and more recently Rangers launched their "Pride over Prejudice" campaign. These initiatives are laudable but clearly much more needs to be done. In recent years football authorities in different parts of the world have made strenuous efforts to stamp out racist behaviour at football matches. The problem has not been eliminated but it has been much reduced. In Scotland a similar concerted effort is needed by our football authorities, supported where appropriate by the police, in relation to sectarian behaviour. Until sectarianism in football is dealt with we should keep reminding Rangers and Celtic of the closing words of James Shaw's report: "If you're a doctor or nurse in accident and emergency in the west of Scotland it pays to keep close tabs on the progress of the Old Firm, not with a sense of mounting excitement as the next game approaches, but with a sense of mounting dread."

Yet despite this type of violence some commentators argue that sectarianism is no longer a major social problem in Scotland. They point to the fact that mixed marriages between Protestants and Catholics have become commonplace, to falling church attendances, to the progress which Catholics have made in the professions and in Scottish society generally and to the absence of discrimination against Catholics in housing and in the workplace. These statements may be true but week after week Nil by Mouth receives a steady flow of telephone calls from teachers, from community groups, from youth workers, all looking for help and support in tackling sectarian issues which confront them daily in the course of their work. Many of these issues may be relatively low level involving verbal abuse of some kind. Every so often, however, the problem escalates and violence follows. Frankly it is irrelevant whether the perpetrators understand the doctrinal differences between various branches of the Christian faith or even whether they ever put in an appearance at church or chapel. They think of themselves and each other as Catholics or Protestants and divide into their opposing camps. Sectarianism is about attitudes and prejudices. It's what many people encounter daily in the workplace, in the pub, in the street and of course at football matches. It's real and in my view it continues to have a widespread and corrosive effect on many aspects of Scottish life.

One of Nil by Mouth's tenets is that everyone should take responsibility for the language they use and the way they behave. Telling a sectarian joke in the pub – or indeed laughing at or just listening to it – may seem relatively harmless. But arguably it's the start of a chain, a long chain which can end in violence and even death. The danger is that the extreme bigots, the ones who perpetrate the sickening violence, imagine that people who laugh at sectarian jokes or sing sectarian songs at football matches must also support more physical expressions of bigotry.

For many people the simple answer to sectarianism is to abolish Catholic schools. Anyone who comments on this topic has to tread carefully. A quick glance at the letters page in the *Herald* every time the subject is raised reveals what an emotive issue it is, particularly in the west of Scotland. It may be that if our politicians and educationalists were starting today with a blank sheet of paper to create a new school system in Scotland they would end up with something very different from what we currently have. But that's not where we are. The reality is that provision of state-funded Catholic schools is enshrined in the 1918 Education Act and it would take primary legislation to abolish them. In the 2003 elections to the Scottish Parliament none of the major political parties put forward such a policy and I cannot see that position changing in the foreseeable future.

There is, however, a legitimate question about whether Scotland's system of non-denominational and Catholic schools, which keeps children from different religious backgrounds apart, encourages ignorance and suspicion. It is the possibility that such division is fuelling the problem that has led to increasing interest in the concept of campus-sharing. Where non-denominational and Catholic schools exist side by side both schools share resources where appropriate and provide opportunities for children to mix. In Glasgow over the next few years we are going to see a huge programme of new primary school building and I hope that everyone involved in the planning of this exercise will consider campus-sharing options wherever possible. In the absence of campus-sharing I would like to see every non-denominational school in the west of Scotland twinned with its neighbouring Catholic school with head teachers being strongly encouraged to promote joint activities between the schools.

Since his appointment as First Minister Jack McConnell has demonstrated his willingness to face up to Scotland's sectarian problems. One of Nil by Mouth's original objectives was about giving power to the courts to impose increased sentences where offences could be shown to have been motivated by sectarianism. This power already exists in relation to offences motivated by race and it seemed to us to be entirely appropriate that the courts should have the same power in relation to offences motivated by sectarianism. The First Minister made clear his support for this position and after long debate the Justice Committee examining the proposed change in the law agreed to recommend it. The new law came into force in June 2003. What now needs to happen is that the police and the prosecuting authorities apply the new law vigorously by presenting relevant evidence on motivation to the courts. One of the key advantages of the new law is that, if applied properly, it will allow detailed statistics on sectarian crime to be collected and analysed for the first time.

At the same time as that change in the law was being debated the Scottish Executive established a cross-party working group of MSPs to look at the issue of religious hatred in Scotland. The group published its report in December 2002 with twelve specific recommendations for action. Some of these have been overtaken by the above change in the law; others relate to the need for more research into, and the gathering of more statistical information about, religious hatred; and others suggest various measures to tackle sectarian behaviour at football matches. During the consultation period Nil by Mouth responded by welcoming the report, broadly agreeing with its recommendations and making a further twelve recommendations of our own. The report and the responses to it are with ministers for consideration and I look forward to an early announcement of important policy initiatives.

Whilst all of that was going on in the Scottish Parliament, Glasgow City Council commissioned a survey on sectarianism in Glasgow. The results of the survey by NFO System Three, published in January of this year, did not make comfortable reading. The key findings were that:

Sixty-five per cent of people surveyed believed there was a serious problem of sectarian violence in Glasgow;

Seventy-one per cent said that using sectarian language was common;

Seventy-seven per cent said that sectarian jokes were very or quite common;

Twenty-five per cent believed that sectarian views influenced job decisions;

More than fifty per cent thought that Orange walks should be banned;

the rivalry between Rangers and Celtic was most commonly seen as the way Glasgow's sectarian divide was sustained.

Glasgow City Council deserves credit for commissioning the survey but it now has to show real commitment by producing a concerted political response to the issues which have been raised. One practical development in Glasgow has been the banning of the sale of sectarian and para-military paraphernalia close to football grounds. Street traders who breach this ban can expect to lose their licences and it will be interesting to see how effectively the ban is enforced.

It is clear that at both national and local level Scotland's politicians have begun to engage with the debate on sectarianism. They understand, I am sure, that there is no quick fix. Eliminating sectarianism in Scotland will take sustained commitment over at least twenty years. We have to start with school children – and the younger the better. With the help of teachers, Nil by Mouth has developed a number of workshops and teaching materials which can be used with children between the ages of seven and fourteen, helping them to think about diversity and the importance of showing respect for the beliefs of other people. We ask them in particular to think about the language they use when talking about people who are different from them. Encouragingly, some neighbouring non-denominational and Catholic primary schools have requested joint workshops. We have also been working with educationalists to develop a specific training programme for teachers and youth workers to help them cope with day-to-day sectarian issues in their work.

For decades there seems to me to have been a conspiracy of silence about the issue of sectarianism in Scottish schools. I remember reading my own children's projects on Martin Luther King and the civil rights movement in the United States, the rise and fall of apartheid in South Africa, issues of sex equality and so on. What they did not discuss at school was sectarianism in their own country nor indeed did they learn anything about thirty years of troubles in Northern Ireland. I remember my children paying school visits to the local Mosque and the Hindu temple but never to a Catholic church. What are we afraid of? How can we expect children to understand and deal with issues if we don't give them the tools to help them do it?

Shortly after Nil by Mouth came into being, the City of Glasgow Education Department suggested looking at some sort of joint application to the Millennium Commission. From that initial discussion a partnership was established comprising Nil by Mouth, Glasgow City Council, the Archdiocese of Glasgow, the Glasgow Presbytery of the Church of Scotland and Rangers and Celtic football clubs. Together we successfully applied to the Millennium Commission for a grant of £400,000 spread over three years which could be used to make awards to people undertaking some innovative form of anti-sectarian activity. The scheme called "Sense over Sectarianism" (SOS for short) was launched in October 2001 and to date over sixty-five awards have been made for a very wide variety of projects. One of my favourite projects involved a school janitor in Glasgow who applied to SOS because he was fed up with the level of sectarian abuse being exchanged by primary school children in neighbouring Catholic and non-denominational schools. He received a grant to start a joint football team drawn from both these schools. After initial hesitation from some parents the janitor got the project up and running with training sessions taking place on a mixed basis in both schools. The idea was very simple but reports indicate that there has been a marked reduction in sectarian behaviour amongst the children concerned. At a micro level these types of project can make a significant difference and when SOS comes to an end in a few months' time Nil by Mouth will be asking the Scottish Executive to fund a successor scheme.

Overall I believe some modest progress has been made in recent years. After many years of being swept under the carpet, the issue of sectarianism is at least being acknowledged now and discussed by our political leaders. The vast majority of Scottish people believe that religious bigotry and intolerance should have no part to play in twenty-first century Scotland and want to see an end to sectarianism. It is up to all of us to ensure that work towards that objective continues in the years to come.

Part III: The Way We Live

Mental Health

Norma Bennie

"Society should be judged by the way it treats its mentally ill"
Golda Meir

Huge advances have been made over the last century in the understanding and treatment of mental illness. No longer are those who are mentally ill chained to public railings, starved or burned to death. We now know that mental disorder is an illness, that it can now be classified, diagnosed and treated. We have experts in the field who can identify when a person's actions are due to a mental illness. Advances in psychology and psychiatric medicine have made most conditions treatable and early diagnosis possible, but sadly it appears that we have not made the same advances in people's perception of mental illness. Mental health, however, has been described as how people, communities and organisations think and feel about themselves and their experience of well-being rather than just an absence of mental illness.

Treatment and care of mental illness is left very much in the hands of the health and social services. In our lifetime we have witnessed the closure of large asylums on the understanding that people with mental illness should be treated within their own communities in small accessible facilities, in many cases attached to district general hospitals. One of the aims of these changes was to integrate mental illness into general medicine and by doing so help to break down the stigma and rejection felt by those who have a mental illness. In Scotland we were more hesitant to fully embrace the concept of Care in the Community. When it was first advocated many hospitals in England rapidly closed down, and the patients were "rehabilitated" into the community, in some cases with disastrous effects. There were instances of patients being left in the care of poorly trained landladies, social services were overstretched and those who were abandoned in the community often deteriorated to the point of requiring hospital care again, but there were fewer hospitals available to take them in. The very high profile case of Christopher Clunis – a schizophrenic discharged into the community with no formal follow up, became more ill and killed Jonathan Zito, a stranger to him, in a random, frenzied attack of which he had no recollection – demonstrated clearly where Care in the Community, as it was provided then, did not work.

Following that case the Care Programme Approach was introduced to all psychiatric services, which assured that a named person would be in charge of each person's care before, during and after discharge. This system, combined with social and personal care, ensures that once a person has been successfully diagnosed and treated, they can be maintained in the community and most can eventually fully recover from their illness to play a full part in society again. Most parts of the jigsaw of care have been identified and addressed but one vital factor remains – the role of society in accepting people with mental illness. People are able to manage through the trauma of becoming ill, can recognise the implications, are willing to undergo treatment, can plan their rehabilitation and future goals; but if they are the subject of ridicule, exclusion and rejection they will never fully recover. Their self-confidence, self esteem and sense of worth depends on acceptance by their relatives, friends, colleagues and the general public. A recent study at the University of California identified that the pain of rejection is just as real as a broken leg. Feelings of hurt affect the same region of the brain that deals with physical pain. There is now evidence to show what many people have felt for years, that to be considered different, "an outcast", makes people experience intense heartache and sorrow from which many never recover.

The media are considered to be the "mouth and ears of the people". Not only do they express opinions which they feel are in line with public opinion but as we know they also mould opinion. We must never under-estimate the power of the media and the influence that the press, radio, television and films have on the public. The recent adoption of Arnold Schwarzenegger as governor of California is a case in point. He dispensed justice in the *Terminator* films. In these he was indestructible, dealing swiftly and effectively with enemies: just the sort of person the American public want as their governor and a clear demonstration of how public opinion can be influenced.

During Mental Health Week, the BBC chose to screen two anti-mental health films, *Silence of the Lambs* and *Me Myself Irene*. *Silence of the Lambs* is a fictional portrayal of someone who commits grossly violent and degrading acts and is portrayed as mentally ill. The story line was not taken from real cases and was purely fictional, but is an uninformed public able to make these distinctions? *Me Myself Irene* was a cheaply humorous portrayal of someone who "flipped" when he stopped taking his medication, a "good guy" becoming a "bad guy". The film ridiculed the symptoms of schizophrenia in an inaccurate and scathing way which is hurtful to those who have the illness and created a negative influence on the public opinion of mental health, encouraging people to make fun of those who have the illness. Perhaps it also discouraged young people who are experiencing psychological symptoms from seeking help, thus driving them into further feelings of rejection and despair.

Not only do the media and film industries demonise and ridicule mental illness: so do some of those who are elected to represent us. Local councillors and MSPs – how do they perceive mental illness? How do they lead public opinion?

An embarrassing example of prejudice can be found in Scotland at present. Health boards in the West of Scotland are planning to build a secure care unit which would admit patients who require psychiatric care in secure surroundings. Three sites are being considered for the development of a thirty-six bed unit. Public consultation is under way at present in three localities – one of which will house the secure care unit. Public opposition to this proposal has been ferocious. "Not in My Back Yardism" is alive and well. The public have given a clear message that, if a secure care unit is to be built, it will not be near where they live.

Committees have been established, petitions signed, posters printed, leaflets distributed and networks established to ensure that this unit will not be developed in any of the three proposed sites.

The Scottish Parliament has issued a formal press release on the subject which quotes four MSPs who are opposed to the development of the secure unit in their area. The press release uses emotive language to describe the conditions which may be treated there. These conditions are described in criminal terms rather than in terms of illnesses; e.g. rape, murder, arson, and paedophilia. Why not talk about these people being there because they suffer from depression, schizophrenia, mania or obsessive disorder? All these conditions are illnesses which are treatable. The MSPs, in the press release, refer to the proposed patients as "unsavoury characters" and express concern that the unit is being considered "close to local schools and homes for the elderly".

Recent evaluation of another established secure site in England showed that in the last four years only eight patients have absconded. Of these, four returned of their own will, three were found by police after short periods, and only one is known to have committed a crime, a street robbery in central London. These are up-to-date figures, not those of twenty years ago, which may have shown a different picture. The outcome of a recent appeals enquiry stated that "there is no evidence to suggest that the risk posed by an absconding patient is any greater in a suburban area than elsewhere. There is also no evidence that children would be at any greater risk than the population at large. Paedophilia is not a mental disorder. Paedophiles who also have a mental disorder may be treated in a secure unit but they would be a very small proportion of the patient group". The report also stated that "children are best protected by having appropriate arrangements in place for the treatment of mentally disordered offenders".

It is understandable that, if mental illness is associated with crime and violence, the public must feel apprehensive. In a recent appeal against the development of a secure care facility in the UK a briefing note presented evidence that:

the association between mental illness and violence in the community is inaccurate and unsubstantiated;

the presence of a medium secure unit within the local community does not affect crime rates;

people with mental health problems are more likely to harm themselves than others;

it is arguable that public perceptions of fear of crime in relation to the mentally ill can be attributed to biased, inaccurate and sensationalist media reporting and, as such, are unreasonable.

Statistics illustrate that, over the past forty years, there has been a marked increase in homicides but a marked decrease in homicides by those who are not found by the court to have a mental illness. In one study of 2,122 persons involved with the police, only eighty-five (four per cent) exhibited signs of mental distress. The study concluded: "The stereotype of the mentally ill as dangerous is not substantiated." This demonstrates that there is a small risk inherent in current methods of providing care but that is a risk which a civilised, informed society has to bear if mentally disordered offenders are to be offered appropriate treatment.

Far from being violent, dangerous offenders, most people suffering from mental health problems are in fact more likely to become the victims of crime. A MIND survey found that almost half of people with mental health problems had been abused or harassed in public, and that fourteen per cent had been physically assaulted. A quarter of people felt that they were at risk of attack inside their own homes, while over a quarter (twenty-six per cent) were forced to move home because of harassment. Also demonstrated in the MIND survey was the effect that negative attitudes, hostility and rejection can have on individuals with mental illness. Just under a quarter of all respondents had experienced hostility from their neighbours and local communities as a result of media reports. Twenty-six per cent felt frightened and vulnerable as a result of coverage and eight per cent felt suicidal. When asked "Who or what do you blame for this?" sixty per cent blamed media coverage and twenty-two per cent blamed politicians.

Depicting people with mental illness as unpredictable and dangerous influences the individual's attitude to an extent that those who have suffered a mental illness and have recovered are afraid to admit it. Could this in part be due to the prejudices they held before they became ill? Many people have a fear of becoming mentally ill, of "losing their mind", so often a way of dealing with these fears is to joke about it, to deny that it could ever happen to them. There may also be a desire to put the painful episode behind them, to get on with their lives and return to "normality" again.

At recent public protest meetings against the development of the secure unit in the west of Scotland, angry, hostile protesters threatened health board staff with violence. They have thrown articles at staff at meetings and hurled verbal abuse at them. An MSP has had death threats because he refused to side with the protesters. If this is what happens to staff, how do patients and their carers feel? One carer who was due to address a public meeting withdrew because of fear of violence.

In the meantime what is happening to those who need care that is currently being denied them? Some are being treated in inadequate surroundings within existing psychiatric units, others are being held in the State Hospital because there is no viable alternative, some are in prison with a mental illness when they should be receiving care and treatment in a specialised unit, others are receiving no care at all and may be living rough and in despair. Suicide figures in Scotland are increasing each year; people are being driven to take their own lives because adequate care is not available. The public opposition to the development of secure care units is holding back opportunities for treatment for many genuinely ill people who are suffering enough because of their illness but even more because of the rejection by the public and the selfish interests of a vocal few. Those who object may not be aware of the pain they are causing to those who are ill. Posters alongside the venue for a public consultation meeting declare "Welcome to Paedophiles' Paradise" and "No Mini-Carstairs in our village." A recently elected member of the Scottish Parliament announced during a debate that patients were "two tablets away from flipping". What kind of society can treat its sick in this way?

How much responsibility should the media have for influencing public opinion? Why are elected representatives behaving in such an ill-informed, prejudicial, biased manner against people who may be their own constituents? A cheap way to get votes? A way of getting on the bandwagon to court popularity? Why can't Scotland's leaders show the way by treating individuals who are ill with respect? One person in four at some point in their lives will suffer from some form of mental illness. Members of the Scottish Parliament, the media, protesters at public meetings – are they immune? Will they never need care? How would they feel if they had a severe depression and were labelled a "psycho", a "loony" or a "paedo"? Would it not make them more depressed, perhaps to the point of taking their own lives?

If we are to be a forward thinking enlightened society, if we value each other as human beings. let us give those who are mentally ill the best chance of recovery – accept them into your community. Trust those who care for them to look after them. Take responsibility yourself by becoming involved in the public participation in your own health service. Those people who are responsible for public opinion have a duty to be informed and present their views in a reasonable, rational manner while being aware of the consequences of their words and actions on others. There are prisons for those who knowingly commit crimes; the State Hospital at Carstairs will still exist for those who are considered ill and too dangerous to be integrated into society. But there is an urgent need for a secure facility for people who are ill, who may or may not have committed a crime but need the protection of asylum, perhaps from themselves and their own life events but perhaps also from our society. Those who are currently in prison and in the State Hospital are being denied the care and treatment to which they are entitled. The suicide rate of those in prison is six times higher than the general population – a reflection of the distress of people who are denied the opportunity for appropriate care.

Scotland has an opportunity to show others how we approach mental illness. Society should take a lively and informed interest in health matters but should also trust those who are in their payment to provide the best, most effective and safest services for all concerned.

Part IV

Where We Live

The Built Environment
The Natural Environment

Part IV: Where We Live

The Built Environment

John Gerrard

The well-known epitaph to Sir Christopher Wren above his tomb in the crypt of St Paul's Cathedral "Si Monumentum requiris, circumspice", offers sound advice, not just to those immediately responsible for the creation and care of buildings but also, in the wider sense, to us all. Our monuments too arise around us and not for nothing has architecture been dubbed the "inescapable art". Each one of us, in some measure, is responsible for the part of what exists or is planned in Scotland's towns, cities and villages and for what we build in the countryside, even though the direct agents of change and conservation are designers and builders, planners, investors and politicians. The public realm is, in the end, the outcome of our choice at the polling station – if we care enough to vote. The ugly office block comes down ultimately to the shares we may own in the businesses which financed, constructed and occupy it. Sprawling housing estates are the product of our over-willingness to accept, without much question, standards of design, convenience and technology that we would soon scorn when buying a new car.

"Planning" is blamed for much that fails to contribute happily to our physical environment, but unless development is bigger than an individual building project, its bureaucratic control often just enables what is already on the drawing board (or probably computer) and otherwise mostly gains time for some improvement. From my years of working with the Scottish Civic Trust I recall the unexplained pleasure of being thanked by an architect for slanging his design of his building, at the stage of the planning application. It seemed that a cheese-paring client had pushed him into submitting a poor scheme, and that the objections forced a necessary redesign. Which serves to emphasise that the high quality in Scotland's built environment, as elsewhere, depends vastly on good patronage – on who commissions the architecture, street furniture, landscaping and civil engineering and his or her or their ability to recognise the difference between good and mediocre design and to follow the best route to achieve the former, beautifully, on time and to budget.

It is so easy to attack the provider when things go wrong, without considering process. Enter, stage left, the Holyrood saga. I was amongst those instinctively delighted by the choice of Enric Miralles' project from an otherwise less than inspirational bunch. Lord Fraser's enquiry should allow hindsight to kick in more sharply but it is not hard to see the subsequent story as a cautionary object lesson for anyone commissioning change in the built environment. The message should be loud and clear, that the architect's brief must be complete before any detail is drawn up and certainly before any work begins on the ground. Here, instead, is a classic case of more haste, less speed, giving grief all round, sadly tarnishing the name of devolution and giving pause to many of those who yearned for the return of a national Parliament.

What hope then for our built environment, in these early days of the new institution? Regarding its new home, it seems reasonable to hope that it will retain the strength of Miralles' vision sufficiently to stimulate the performance and imagination of the MSPs, staff and public alike, in spite of the awkward problem of fitting so much accommodation into a non-elastic site and the little difficulty of installing an experimental roof in a Scottish climate threatened by even more globally-warmed downpours.

What else has devolution brought to the built environment? For a start, Words, Words, Words, in the shape of the Executive's policy paper on *Culture, Architecture and the Design of Places*. "Joined up thinking" was the founding mantra of this developed administration and if only the merry-go-round of the various ministers responsible for culture, heritage, education and life-long learning had meanwhile stopped for long enough, we might already be seeing more of its impact on the ground. We have to remember, however, that the Westminster administration would never have got us so far, so soon, and that important building and planning projects are not achieved overnight.

The policy for architecture was never the less on the slipway ahead of the launch of the Parliament and it owed much to those already in place in comparable countries such as the Netherlands. Amongst other expectations, it raises the hope that projects paid for by public money will "embrace good design as a means of achieving value for money and sustainable development." Ask those experiencing some of the products of the government's favoured Private Finance Initiative method of procuring public building and one realises that hope must continue to spring eternally.

Fortunately the education aims seem to be more firmly rooted, thanks in part to the Policy's commitment to the Lighthouse Centre for Design and the City, one of the lasting legacies of Glasgow 1999, whose national and international outreach has been boosted by increased support from the Executive. It is just such a pity that the fine idea of creating it out of the redundant *Herald* building has located it up a narrow vennel so that, for those outside the loop, it is not a place one discovers by chance.

Designing Places however, seems the most interesting of these policies. It moves on from the quality of the individual structure to promote the cause of creating and retaining vital and memorable combinations of buildings and, as important, the spaces between them – an art that seems to have been largely lost in post-war Scotland. The aim is to manage this through our planning system, begging the enormous question of how to achieve this when so few professional planners are nowadays trained to think visually and in three dimensions. The jury on the success of all three policies may be out for some time.

Meanwhile a mood of scrutiny and potential change hangs over our Royal Fine Art Commission and Historic Scotland. The former has never been allowed the powers to ensure the abortion or adequate improvement of the many poor projects that come before it and which – see its fascinating website – it frequently excoriates. Recent announcements give hope that the Executive will follow the route taken in England, reforming the Commission as a powerful pro-active champion of good design while sharpening its watchdog's teeth against bad and mediocre projects.

At the same time, Historic Scotland is under heavy review, as every public agency should be from time to time, and it is too soon to be sure if its role or make-up will be significantly changed. Its underfunding has been a frequent source of complaint since the end of the Tory era, which was in fact quite generous to the built heritage. Transparency and accountability have rarely been amongst Historic Scotland's strengths and the voluntary organisations working in the field would be glad to see improvements there, as well as in the resources it is given for the benefit of its properties in care, for its educational and admirable technical work and for its oversight of the built heritage in general. This review has been accompanied, after some heavy lobbying, by the appointment of a new Historic Environment Advisory Council to act as an outside source of guidance and which will presumably hope to contribute some joined-up thinking to the relevant minister. Amongst its priorities it must give urgent attention to the gulf existing between posture and practice in the care for heritage demanded of our local authorities. Far too many are short of, or completely lack, suitably qualified and influential conservation staff. It is almost scandalous that council areas the size of Ayrshire and Perthshire, with their multitude of listed properties and conservation areas, have no in-house experts, working on behalf of the finely worded heritage policies in their statutory development plans and helping their planning committees to follow them with rigour and imagination.

With so much in flux, the National Lottery remains a steady force in the business of funding new arts and heritage building projects, or repairing and renewing the historic building stock and, as important, of encouraging environmental and cultural education. It is hard to recall a time without the Lottery and its benefits or remember that it predates New Labour. A Scottish catalogue of its significant good works on behalf of the built environment, from multi-million pound support for such schemes as the National Gallery's Playfair Project to the provision of a computer for a local heritage group, would already resemble a small phone book.

What more to report? Mostly the world carries on, as before. As decent old buildings disappear through development pressures, neglect, disaster, mischance or criminal intent, more are added to the list by Historic Scotland's assiduous inspectors. Our knowledge of the built heritage grows by research and the publication of new architectural guidebooks, both scholarly and popular. Enthusiasm for that eclectic annual jamboree, Doors Open Day, seems not to diminish. Architectural horrors continue to fall through the leaky aesthetic safety net of the planning system. The unexpected happens, notably in the huge popular appeal of the recent television *Restoration* programmes, which helped the prospects of the Scottish contenders, even though they failed to win, and did no harm at all to the general cause of saving buildings at risk.

Otherwise, time will tell if our Executive's efforts to get to grips with the built environment begin to bear good fruit or merely wither on the Holyrood vine. I was recently asked by a journalist to nominate the most ugly new building in Scotland. A short-list of two in central Glasgow – a cinema and a hotel – came quickly to mind. If the year ahead spares us more of the same, then we may sense a glimmer, at least, of future progress.

Part IV: Where We Live

The Natural Environment

Roger Crofts

Rural Scotland and Scotland's natural environment are usually taken to be synonymous. The Minister for Environment is also responsible for rural development and the key rural economic sectors. Even the new committee structure of the Scottish Parliament seeks to perpetuate this view with the establishment of an Environment and Rural Development Committee. This perspective is erroneous.

Examining who pays for, uses, looks after, and needs rural areas gives broader perspective. There is a multiplicity of legitimate interests: we all have a stake in the environment and most of us have some dependency on "rural Scotland". The debates and actions during 2003 and 2004 clearly back up this point; for example, on national parks, public access and the right to buy land, nature and community conflicts, on agriculture, and on fishing, forestry and tourism. These six topics are elaborated as they affect citizens in rural and urban Scotland.

I must be honest about my own position. I have lived all of my life in urban areas but have worked on rural development and environment issues for decades. I unashamedly argue for better care of our natural environment for its own sake and for the contribution it brings to improving our life chances now and for future generations.

Widening the basis of land ownership

The debate on who should own the land has been a hardy perennial. The new legislation has righted some wrongs without radically changing the face of ownership. Some traditional interests were taken by surprise perhaps because they thought that the ability for communities to register an interest in their local land would never come to fruition, or so they hoped. Equally, it has been seen by some enlightened owners and some more courageous communities as a great opportunity to do things differently. This reform is far from the radical change that some demanded and others feared. Without a real sense of purpose and leadership from communities and without the support of funds, largely from the National Lottery, we should expect only a limited amount of change of ownership to local communities. Nevertheless, the reform is in tune with demands for restoring traditional rights and responsibilities elsewhere and is a genuine attempt to deliver social justice to rural communities.

The celebrations of ten years of local ownership success, for example in Assynt, appear to indicate that success can be achieved. But some of the media hype may be masking more deep-seated issues. It is very difficult to achieve commitment and agreement from all members of the community to secure the success of community ownership in the longer term.

Making public access legitimate

The passing of the access provisions of the Land Reform (Scotland) Act 2003 has to be one of the great social achievements of the Scottish Parliament. Scotland finally catching up with its Nordic neighbours has to be a cause of celebration wherever you live and work. Can anyone believe that these reforms would have been passed so easily through the Westminster parliament? I doubt it. Over a century of campaigning by politicians and citizens has resulted in a formal statutory right to be on private land for informal recreation and access, but with legitimate safeguards to property and privacy. The stigma of being potentially in a state of trespass, indeed whether there was a law of trespass or whether there was a *de facto* right of access, have all been resolved by the 2003 Act.

Owners of land and the access bodies are to be congratulated for bringing the issues into the open and agreeing resolutions. The Access Forum has played a significant role in defining legislative change and codifying good practice. This facilitative approach, involving all of the interests, to debate and resolve issues on which there are many divergent perspectives is a good model.

To owners who fear that their privacy will be lost and providing access will be too costly, my message is not to worry as I and many others like me welcome the clarification of where we can and cannot go with legitimacy and how we should respect the rights and livelihoods of owners. For the reforms to be really successful more public and private resources are needed and greater effort is required to develop path networks.

Celebrating the special national places

One week after the vote for the Scottish Parliament in 1997 Donald Dewar announced that Scotland would have National Parks. The Loch Lomond and The Trossachs National Park was established in 2002 and The Cairngorms National Park in 2003. They are recognition of Scotland's new national status and, at long last, put us on a par with most other nations. This is rightly a cause for celebration locally and nationally with a positive supporting chorus from the international community.

Scotland's National Parks have social and economic development roles alongside the traditional roles of nature and landscape conservation and public enjoyment. Ensuring that all of the purposes are delivered is the most important challenge to the park authorities; these areas are not just bastions of nature protection and not just tourism development areas, or enterprise zones.

There are three other tests of success. First, they must make a difference in restoring land degraded over many generations by overgrazing and other forms of mismanagement. This will require changes in the agriculture support regime from food production to environmental stewardship. And it will require a more effective approach to the management of deer by the Deer Commission for Scotland and by owners and managers to ensure that the numbers are finally brought in balance with the carrying capacity of the deer range.

Second, they must make a difference by engaging local interests in the governance of the parks and in ensuring that they benefit socially and financially from its existence. This will require building the capacity of locals to participate, and providing positive incentives to locals for business development and other activities.

And, third, they must make a difference in balancing effectively national and local interests. It is curious that local interests predominantly manage our new national parks: surely they are for the benefit of the nation as a whole, and that includes visitors to Scotland. If they descend into parochialism because of the imbalance of local interests on the authority and if they ignore the wider cultural, aesthetic and environmental values, then that will be a major disappointment.

I find it misguided that much of the argument has not been about these big issues but about boundaries and planning powers. For sure the extension of the Loch Lomond and The Trossachs National Park into Cowal, and the failure to extend The Cairngorms National Park into Highland Perthshire were unjustified on any objective grounds. The argument about planning powers seems to be dictated by the English situation and bears little relation to the reality that most of the management issues which the park authorities should deal with are well outside the ambit of the planning system.

Resolving conflicts between people and nature

One of the issues which divides rural and urban Scotland is the protection of its wildlife. Much of the opposition is not unreasonably based in rural Scotland where wildlife protection is perceived to be imposed upon owners of land and is also perceived to disadvantage rural communities economically. The rise of various bodies purporting to represent rural interests is a manifestation of this divide. The implementation of the EU

Habitats and Species, and Birds Directives by the government through its agency Scottish Natural Heritage, has caused debate, argument, opposition and legal challenges. That Scotland has progressed so effectively, given the extent of the area and the number of sites and the *dirigiste* European approach, is the recognition of the importance of Scotland from a European perspective, the pragmatic approach of many owners and managers, the environmental bodies who quite rightly pressed the case for more areas and greater speed, and is also testimony to the skills of staff in Scottish Natural Heritage. One key ingredient in making progress has been the implementation of schemes under the Natural Care banner by SNH to provide positive financial support to owners in the management of these important sites. It is pleasing therefore that these positive approaches are to be formalised in legislation just put before Parliament and that the outmoded, unfriendly and uneconomic approaches of compensation for doing nothing are about to disappear.

The new legislation and support mechanisms, along with opportunities for wildlife tourism, may bring benefits not only to wildlife but also to those who have the privilege to care for it on their land, those who wish to visit it, and the rural communities in the surrounding areas.

Farming is more than food production

One of the major issues affecting rural areas and the environment has been the future of agriculture and, more particularly, the future role of farmers. Urban communities are also interested given their support as taxpayers for rural areas, especially support for agricultural production and for maintaining "the fabric of the countryside". These issues were brought into sharp perspective by the foot and mouth disease epidemic. This had a devastating effect on farmers' incomes in the affected areas, ruined generations of livestock development, raised legitimate concerns about some animal husbandry practices, and most significantly brought to the public's attention the importance of access to the countryside for the tourism industry. Thankfully the epidemic is over and the control measures lifted. The lessons documented in the many reports should be taken heed of so that any recurrence is minimised.

New schemes for supporting environmentally friendly agriculture, under the Rural Stewardship Scheme, have been widely welcomed by farmers and by environmental bodies. It is clear from the affirmative response from all constituencies that the long-standing Environmentally Sensitive Areas schemes have been successful in galvanising action for the environment and are good value for money. Many habitats, especially wetlands, and many species, particularly farmland birds, have benefited, although the degree of success is not as much as is needed according to environmentalists. In addition, it is hoped that the priority given to the Organic Aid scheme will bring benefits to soil quality and bio-safety of food products. Funding for agri-environment work is much less than is required to overcome the effects of long-term intensive production driven by UK and EU food supply policy. It is essential that substantially more resources be provided for environmental schemes on farms: a point which now unites all of the constituencies of interests.

A welcome step has been the debate about the future of Scottish agriculture and the production of *A Forward Strategy for Scottish Agriculture* and the report of the sub-committee on agriculture and the environment. The implementation of these reports should stimulate alternative activities for farmers, improve the quality assurance of food produced for the consumer, help to develop new markets, and meet some of the environmental targets. It is, however, disappointing that the more radical and progressive proposals put forward for England and Wales have been so unthinkingly rejected by the Agriculture Minister and the Farmers Union in Scotland. At times, it seems that Scottish agriculture has to proceed at the pace of the slowest in the ministry rather that at a pace which progressive farmers and the thinking groups within rural and urban communities are seeking.

No doubt the agreement on the Mid-Term Review of the Common Agricultural Policy will provoke demand for a different deal and slower implementation for Scotland, when what is needed is for the role of farmers to be recognised and supported beyond the production of high quality food. There is little point in just removing the financial support for food production and assuming that farmers and therefore their role in the countryside will be safeguarded. New measures and the re-direction of funds to support them are urgently required. More recognition for farmers' role in protecting and improving wildlife, in helping to implement the new access laws, in maintaining the look of the countryside, in helping to achieve the implementation of the new water management legislation on farms, are all part of this wider role.

Fishing, forestry and tourism changing direction

There have been challenges for the three other main economic activities in rural areas. These have affected both rural and urban communities. There can be no doubt that the white fish industry is in crisis. The concerns for the financial viability of the businesses and the longevity of the dependent communities are issues which should concern all citizens. The closure of the North Sea cod fishery to Scottish boats is but the most significant in an industry which seems to be very efficient in upgrading its capacity to find and catch fish, but not very effective in maintaining the balance between natural recruitment to the fish stock and the catching capacity of the vessels.

In addition, there are many occasions when fish that are protected or their quotas severely restricted are caught as by-catch and then discarded. New stocks are difficult to find, and fishing those few in remote parts of our waters, for instance on the Darwin Mounds off the Outer Hebrides, have caused damage to the unique cold water corals to the extent that a new solution of banning fishing from the area is being developed. Most significantly, there remains weakness in the market for fish, although there are welcome signs, albeit anecdotal, that the large supermarket chains are seeking to increase sales of fish. There remains competition from the aquaculture industry. Farm-produced salmon is now at an affordable price, and despite many concerns and scares about husbandry, neither the regulators nor the public seem to be deterred from buying its products. Other species are at an advanced stage in the development of farming and will no doubt reach the market in increasing quantities in the future.

However, none of these developments brings any salvation to deeper water fishermen and their dependent human communities. It is not surprising that we have seen protests about the closure of fisheries, and the wholesale decommissioning of boats. These measures do not solve the economic and social problems or the fish recruitment and supply issues. At the time of writing, the latest assessments from scientists indicate that the decline in white fish stocks, particularly North Sea cod, is continuing. Many recognise that the science is not perfect but this does not absolve fisheries ministers, fishing industry leaders and fishermen from ignoring it or claiming that their own observations are more precise. Indeed, much of the root of the present problem lies in the naive approach over the years that preserving catch levels is more important than conserving the stock itself. As a result the level of recruitment to the fish stock necessary to sustain the industry in the longer term has not been achieved.

It is difficult to see alternative roles for fishermen using their skills. However, developing a range of methods to allow stocks to rebuild are needed: areas where fish spawn and breed should be identified and closed to fishing – a method used successfully in other countries – stricter controls on by-catch of those species not sought, draconian controls on those crews who flaunt the rules by landing illegally caught fish, and further improvements in surveillance and enforcement of illegal activity by less use of ships and more use of satellite tracking.

Given the low price of timber on the world market, the forestry sector has not had an easy time. However, we are seeing the benefits of the substantial long-term investment in forestry by the state, both in maintaining a supply of home-grown soft wood to the various processing factories and also diversifying the use of the afforested areas for wider public benefit. Particularly significant has been the recognition of the role which the national forest estate plays in biodiversity conservation. Felled areas are now left unplanted, native trees retained, and native species planted. The semi-natural pine, oak and ash woods in particular have benefited from removal of non-native species in recognition of their unique position in Europe. There has also been further extension of the use of state forests for both informal quiet recreation and for noisier activities. All of these activities have been put in a more strategic context with the impressive forestry strategy for Scotland, led by the Forestry Commission.

In the tourism industry many believe that the lack of leadership from the government agency visitScotland has been at the root of Scotland's failure to compete effectively in both domestic and internal markets. This strikes me as blaming the messenger when the standards of service in the industry remain poor, and when brochure production seems to be more important than providing visitors with what they want.

The Area Tourist Board structure is convoluted and gives all the appearance of an industry that wishes to stay firmly in a dependence culture rather than improving the range of opportunities, exploiting the strengths which Scotland naturally has, and significantly improving service standards. Admittedly the industry has gone through a bad period with the effects of foot and mouth disease, with the after effects of "9/11", and with the effective competition from Sunbelt destinations. But blaming the agency rather than getting on with the job of looking after visitors has not been the way to succeed.

Conclusion

Some new alliances have emerged, such as forestry and access, environment and tourism, urban professionals and remoter rural communities. Inevitably also some of the longer standing issues remain despite progress: the people versus nature debate, the failure to capitalise sufficiently on the sustainable development ethos to bridge the gaps, the myopic attention to fishing communities rather than the long-term sustainable management of the natural resource of the marine biomass, finding new roles for farmers which are likely to be financially viable and have community support. Both urban and rural communities have a legitimate stake and are more interdependent than many admit.

Part V

Culture of Scotland

Literature
Film
Art
Theatre
Poetry
Sport

Part V: Culture of Scotland

Literature

Tom Hubbard

When you're in another country, Scotland has a way of looming at you suddenly and unexpectedly. Last January I was in Bern, Switzerland, undertaking research for BOSLIT, the online Bibliography of Scottish Literature in Translation. On my last evening, returning from the Swiss National Library to the hotel, I passed a bookshop window from which A. L. Kennedy gazed into the dark street. A German-language magazine had recently interviewed her, and I returned to Scotland with more up-to-date information than I'd anticipated. Eleven months on, as I survey the Scottish literary crop of 2003, I'm bound to wonder how much of it will travel and what will happen to it when it gets there, wherever "there" may be. Already, though, we can obtain a sampling of possible answers, thanks to the web, that giftie which gives us the power "tae see oorsels as ithers see us".

Not only in Scotland, but in Britain as a whole, Andrew O'Hagan's novel *Personality* (Faber) was received as a barely-disguised fictional account of the gruesome career of Lena Zavaroni, child prodigy and adult anorexic. O'Hagan's Maria Tambini, a daughter of the chippie, is groomed for the stardom not readily associated with the promenades of Bute, is taken up by Hughie Green's *Opportunity Knocks*, becomes more consumed than consuming: the pattern is familiar to anyone aware of the real-life template. The *Denver Post*'s reviewer, however, didn't mention Zavaroni and had probably never heard of her; his real-life analogue was a fellow-American, Michael Jackson. An Australian journalist, Tony Baker, was aware of the Zavaroni controversy but stressed that Antipodean readers, alert to their own cultural signals, would surely respond to O'Hagan's take on "the Faustian bargain of celebrity". It's instructive to encounter responses free of the baggage associated with that institution "contemporary Scottish fiction". All too often the phrase suggests cutting-edge, gritty, urban, working-class etc., with the subtext that any setting outside the central belt is uncool and won't win us pals among the opinion-formers in London and New York. Hence the spectacle of the promotion of the dour by the slick, a ScotLit as narrowly defined by an alliance of the PC-left and the market-right. While we are appeased by predictable right-on gestures, our culture risks being reduced to niche product. Alternatively we can undertake the necessary fieldwork and try to determine how far our writers, canonised or not, represent the totality of contemporary Scotland from Dumfries to Shetland.

Scottish city fiction works best when it doesn't take itself too earnestly, as witness the satirical novels of Christopher Brookmyre. Agnes Owens' new volume, *Bad Attitudes* (Bloomsbury), consists of two novellas. The first one features a grotesque assemblage of warring neighbours, a dodgy ageing bachelor obsessed with his dead mother, travelling folk, and a social worker who maintains that "all my clients are normal; it's their lives that aren't." To the east, and to the tormented schemie, Jools, in Paul Reed's first novel *The One* (Crescent Books): a schizophrenic's odyssey through Edinburgh, offset by humour, albeit of the blackest. Back west, I was captivated by much in the short-story anthology *A Fictional Guide to Scotland* (OpenInk), particularly Les Wood's *Nodding Off*, the unpretentious tragic-comic tale of Simon, forever wheeling his handicapped brother up Sauchiehall Street, unable to share in the financial and sexual fulfilment which others take for granted.

On one celebrated instance in our literature, Edinburgh was disguised as London, one mask among many in a study of the gentility of evil. In *Dr Jekyll and Mr Hyde*, Robert Louis Stevenson produced a rare example of a late nineteenth-century urban Scottish novel, and without making it too obvious that he was doing so. Ian Rankin has inherited RLS's mantle in his explorations of their precipitous, duplicitous city. *A Question of Blood* (Orion), the latest case for DI Rebus, isn't lacking in the gruff wit of Rankin's native county. Encountering the most recent denizens of Cockburn Street, Rebus remarks that, when he was their age, the only Goths he knew of were the community pubs of that name in the Fife mining towns. It's a tart juxtaposition of contemporary in-your-face style statements with old-fashioned provincial integrity. Yet as the novel moves between Edinburgh and South Queensferry, we're reminded of provincial Scotland's curtain-twitching tensions. When Rankin revealed that his new book would begin with a shooting at a Scottish school, he was accused of exploiting the Dunblane massacre. Actually, two of the victims are private-school adolescents, not primary school children; there is no attempt to replicate what happened in March 1996. Nevertheless, Rankin's police at one point study a photo of Thomas Hamilton – "No one thought him exceptional" – and we could hardly expect this author to go coy on contemporary actualities. In the chronicle of recent years, Dunblane was a more significant event than the opening of the Scottish Parliament. During 2003, Val McDermid, Rankin's fellow crime-supremo – and fellow-Fifer – brought out *The Distant Echo* (HarperCollins), its murder set in St Andrews around 1978, its mystery occupying the quarter-century since then.

The phrase "State of Scotland" in the twenty-first century curiously echoes the "Condition of England" in the early nineteenth, when novelists such as Elizabeth Gaskell and Charlotte Brontë in *Shirley* pursued their enquiries in the provincial North. True, that was a time and place of heavy industrialisation, whereas by the 1990s our Scottish coalfields had been reclaimed as country parks and heritage sites. Nevertheless, we can chart profound social and cultural change even in our smaller communities – indeed, even the word "communities" has evaded re-examination, as if we feared that it might have become drained of meaning. So let's turn to the seriously under-valued Lorn Macintyre, by now a veteran of the literary scene, and his new collection *Tobermory Days* (Argyll Publishing). Shelved in the non-fiction section of my habitual Edinburgh bookshop, it's actually a series of short stories and sketches tracing the quietly significant changes in the eponymous Mull town. It's the kind of book at which Scots and Americans excel: the pieces have in common a core of recurrent characters – in this case, a Gaelic-loving bank manager and his family – but each individual story introduces one or more new personalities with an incident to match. In the US they use the phrase "local color" to describe this genre; in a Scottish context that would suggest the kailyard, but Macintyre succeeds in honouring island life without resorting to cosiness. The north American parallel is apt, given Mull's history of emigration across the ocean; at key points that past haunts the present and the future, not least as regards the uncertain state of Gaelic language and culture. The tales are largely set in the 1950s, but we receive them largely via the consciousness of Marsaili, the banker's daughter, who has "emigrated" to Glasgow; in adulthood she makes a return trip to the island but regrets it, even as she drives off the ferry. Home is home no more.

One of the more interesting newcomers is Suhayl Saadi, born in 1961, who has staked his fictional territory in Glasgow's Southside; he's Scots-Asian even in language (prompting us to speculate on possible future registers for our literature, once the children of new immigrants reach writing age). There are signs, though, that he will resist containment as a "Glasgow writer", and in the short story *Braga*, set in Orkney, he emulates the late George Mackay Brown on his home turf. The piece is striking for its protagonist's realisation that, at a time when he's taking stock of his life, he has come almost as far north as it's possible to go: "But move on where? He had come to the end of the land – beyond the end, actually – because, really, where else might an extreme situation present itself? Change came only through such extremes."

Søren Kierkegaard, the great philosopher of the Scandic north, would have endorsed that insight. The individual is poised, tremblingly, for a leap into the unknown. In Scotland, though, many of us go beyond an individual to a social existentialism. We seek not so much salvation as belonging, and yes, in the process we relish the extremes: when we're in Scotland, we long to get the hell out; once expatriated, we want to go home again, if indeed we *can* go home again, to echo the American novelist Thomas Wolfe. We're often greener than the grass on the other side.

O'Hagan's Maria Tambini loses her "personality" partly because she can't go home again. John Burnside's *Living Nowhere* (Cape) turns on the friendship between members of Scottish and Latvian families living in Corby, the new town which grew around a steelworks in middle England. Their sense of rootlessness is widespread: "People here were always talking about *home*, and they always meant some other place." If there was no prospect of retiring there, they'd arrange "for their bodies to be taken back to Dunfermline, or Cracow, or Paisley". This echoes O'Hagan's description of a Lochgilphead nursing home filled with old people of various European ethnicities, including Maria's; dementia augments their condition of estrangement.

In the major triumph of the year, *Joseph Knight* (Fourth Estate), James Robertson offers us a historical novel and more; he traces the life of a black slave, owned by a Scottish planter in Jamaica, and obliged to accompany his master on the latter's permanent return to his estate some miles from Dundee. When Knight absconds with a servant girl and establishes his own family in the city's Hilltown, an irate Lord Wedderburn is determined to recover his property. Knight, dramatically, takes his bid for freedom to the Edinburgh courts and wins. He and his family resettle in the Fife coastal coalfield, at Wemyss; he becomes one of the colliers, who are as black as he is. Solidarity might have called forth sentimentality, but Robertson's touch is assured. Snatched in turn from West Africa, the Caribbean, and Dundee, Knight has at last discovered home; the work is far more back-breaking and dangerous than that of a domesticated slave, but it's coexistential with a realm of choice. "Others would buy him a drink, or leave a few rabbits poached from the laird's parks. *That* was life, that was heroism: friendship, and trust, and once in a while a little stolen delight."

In principle we shouldn't exclude Scottish writers resident outside Scotland. Those who are London-based, for example, write about the old country in ways that wouldn't occur to those of us still here. This can spell both good and ill for the work of expats. Dumfries-born Alison Fell's *Tricks of the Light* (Doubleday) has the air of a sophisticated, writerly novel, but for all its psychological probing I felt unconvinced by its middle-aged protagonist, the theatre artist Broom, and her several love affairs.

She's supposed to be a sometime Scottish leftie – Fell herself was formerly published by the feminist house Virago – but a rather pathetic mellowing eases her attraction to obnoxious City types, such as Lockhart who flies to his Highland estate ("the soil of another country") where he and his family delight in patronising the locals, and Micky, a thirtyish advertising exec whom she meets in the French Alps. After arguing too charmingly with the smug Micky, Broom feels embarrassed about her origins peeping through: "Thus the Scots after a glass or two, she thought: on fire with our lost causes, our missionary passions." What she sees in the wee nyaff is beyond me, but then I'm not a fiftysomething woman. It would be good to see Fell revisiting the scenes of her early work, such as *The Bad Box* (1987), once again writing *of* rather than *about* Scotland.

In Heligoland (Cape) her near-contemporary, Shena Mackay, mines a Muriel Spark-like vein. This shortish novel presents a gaggle of frightfully south-London eccentrics who inhabit a house designed, in the 1930s, to resemble a giant shell. Into their Utopian community, as housekeeper, scuttles Rowena Snow, a much put-upon soul of Scots-Asian stock. In spite of her fondness for MacDiarmid's lines on the little white rose of Scotland, she has lacked the oomph to return to the old country from which she was dislocated in childhood. Eventually she does contemplate a brief trip, but Scotland's role as her own personal Utopia just isn't strong enough; she's too set in the ways of the shell-folk.

Language, that intimate talisman of identity, is rarely far away from consideration of Scottish writing. Some have claimed that the recent surge of prose in Scots is due to the influence of Irvine Welsh, but the pedigree goes much further back than the blow-jobs/no-jobs axis of metrofiction. Anne Donovan's *Buddha Da* (Canongate) is reminiscent rather of Alan Spence; it's a gentle but gallus novel related by a Glaswegian girl whose painter-decorator father confounds his family by telling them that he's become a Buddhist. Even more alarmingly, he introduces his lamas to the Maryhill milieu. One woman, surprised on her doorstep, enquires: "Are yous anythin tae dae wi the Mormons?" In due course, Da announces to Ma that he's taking up celibacy. A very different Scots

– Aberdeenshire Doric – is handled with equal panache by Sheena Blackhall in *Loon*, her contribution to the two-novella volume *Double-Heider* (Itchy Coo) which also carries *The Girnin Gates* by westerner Hamish MacDonald. Blackhall's Donnie Paterson – the loon – suffers from parental break-up, a dressy house-proud maternal gran, and much else. He has a tendency to get into trouble through no fault of his own. "I discovered fae loons oot aboot that social wirkers in Granny's street wis a rarity, bit roon the Sabban estate a social wirker wis a status symbol, ye wis naethin without ane, some families hid twa or mair, like fridge freezers or TVs." Becoming someone's client, though, promises change: he's sent on a camping trip to the Highlands. His sole sympathetic relative, the paternal granddad whom he visits in the nursing home, has mysterious information which may also help to transform his life.

In the light of mainland Europe's interest in Scotland, one could wish that Scotland displayed more interest in mainland Europe – that as well as being the translated we would become ourselves translators. We have precedents enough, most notably Edwin Morgan. But the commitment involves more than translation, not least a readiness to write Scottishly on non-Scottish themes. Janice Galloway's *Clara* (Cape, 2002) was a breakthrough: it's based on the life of the musician Clara Schumann. In short stories published in magazines over the past year, Ron Butlin has surrealised the lives of European composers, as in *The Fairytale Science Fiction World of Anton Dvorák* (*Cencrastus*, Issue 75). R.L. Stevenson, as ever an inspiration to Scottish internationalism, presented *The Master of Ballantrae* as "a tale which extends over many years and travels into many countries". *Joseph Knight* is such a tale, as is David Nicol's *The Foundations of New Caledonia* (Luath Press), a chunky novel almost entirely composed in a rich, energetic Scots and based on the events surrounding the disastrous Darien venture of 1698-1700. Historical novels, by virtue of present imagination reconstructing past events, help us to obtain the larger view of the contemporary; they challenge our temporal parochialism. Moreover, if they focus on an unfamiliar participant in a familiar historical moment, we find ourselves revising the received wisdom on both the present and the past. This is what Robin Jenkins, now in his nineties, achieves in *Lady Magdalen* (Canongate): the bitterness and bloodiness of the wars of the 1640s are viewed from the perspective of the wife of the Marquis of Montrose. The tragedy is that Magdalen's womanly pacifism is ahead of its time, and ours.

Ali Smith continues to experiment with narrative in her short story collection *The Whole Story* (Hamish Hamilton). She values craftsmanship: "I want to make a book so strong you can hit it with a hammer and it doesn't fall apart." In September a youngish writer (early thirties), Ruaridh Nicoll, brought out his second novel, *Wide Eyed* (Doubleday): an outsider, staying in a fishing village for a short break, finds herself caught up in the aftermath of a boating tragedy.

At BOSLIT we regard much non-fictional writing as worthy to be called literature. An eloquent piece of journalism can resonate more strongly than many a poem or novel. Alasdair Gray's collection, *The Ends of the Tethers* (Canongate), published as recently as mid-October, interested me less for the short stories than for his account of February's anti-war march through Glasgow. Two media folk, Rhona ("the moaner") Cameron and Alistair Moffat published memoirs. Cameron's *Nineteen Seventy-Nine* (Ebury Press) tells you all you need to know about adolescent lesbianism in Musselburgh; inevitably more subdued than Cameron, Moffat in *Homing* (John Murray) relates his childhood in the Borders, and how he chafed against the aggressive parochialism of his father. Readers of the Institute of Contemporary Scotland's journal *The Scottish Review* (September 2003) obtained a foretaste of Kay Carmichael's forthcoming book-length account of her own religiously and socially existentialist journey, *Sin and Forgiveness: New Responses in a Changing World*; the extract was accorded the title *The Lost Homeland*, borrowed from Albert Camus. Kay Carmichael tries to make sense of her West of Scotland upbringing by revisiting writers from a different culture. After all, you need the distance in order to understand your homeland; regaining it takes a bit longer.

Part V: Culture of Scotland

Film

John Izod

Let me be personal about this: there is plenty to celebrate in Scottish cinema. Who in the mid-1980s would have thought it would be possible to say so again? Cinema-going in Britain, according to some experts and a myriad of movie gossips, was being prepared for burial. Audience numbers dropped to the lowest ever recorded, cinemas were closing and for many people the opinion prevailed that home video rental would soon supplant theatrical exhibition because it made for cheaper viewing.

Fast forward to the new century and we find that the recognition by acutely tuned American cinema chains of people's appetite for the shared experience of drama has changed everything. Their managements understand that spectators like to enjoy movies in clean, comfortable auditoria with crystal clear images and sounds of stunning force and range – and that exhibitors can make big money by feeding that appetite. Consider the UGC Renfrew Street in Glasgow, right in the city centre, eighteen screens stacked vertically, regularly drawing long, excited and fast-moving queues served by some ten cash desks. Is it a missed architectural opportunity? Yes – it could have been visually stunning instead of tawdry, its interest mainly confined to the stack of neon-blue lined elevators that level by level open up a fine view across the city. Is it tacky? Yes – the foyers reek of sugar from the Disneyesque fast-serve confectionery stands. They are a bedlam of clashing sound tracks, posters, plasma screens carrying trailers and winking signboards.

But does it provide a good film-going experience? Yes – and the audiences turning out in their hundreds every weekend know it.

Not only is the screening quality excellent, but the programme is more varied than that of many multiplexes. Notably its selections often conflict with those of the GFT just along the street, and it must be providing the older, subsidised venue that has served Glaswegians so well for so long with a new headache.

The single event that dominated the past year in my own life in cinema, as for many film lovers in central Scotland, was the re-opening of the MacRobert Arts Centre at the University of Stirling with a new, long wished-for and purpose-built cinema at its core. Whereas for the previous thirty years film shared a single auditorium with all the other performing arts, we can now enjoy screenings some mornings, most afternoons and every night. Watching a special interest film as we used to in a 500-seat auditorium with perhaps forty other enthusiasts makes the spectator feel exposed and rather alienated. In the new 135-seat venue it's an intimate, warm experience. Films are screened for longer runs and much closer to their release date than used to be the case. Here too sound and vision are wonderfully clear. For me personally as a lecturer in film studies, it has led to the finding, under its crisp light path, of my cinematic home after long years in the wilderness working with inadequate facilities.

The wilderness, now there's a familiar thought! How many accounts have you read describing the marginal, even imperilled state of cinema in Scotland? Justifiable of course, because we *are* on the margins. But how often and how easily in the past newspaper editors have goaded Scottish film-makers into injudicious lament. It was always hard to resist the temptation of doubting that these could be people of incandescent talent as, year-in, year-out, in full public gaze they cheerlessly set about making things worse for themselves. It would not have been so bad (not worse than at the level of the "whingeing pom" of my colonial youth) if they had rested content with picturing the daily – and real enough – miseries of their under-funded professional existence. But to play out the corrosive squabbles typical of a tiny community that feels itself under threat and to do this under the delusion that such tensions are unique to Scotland – that seemed to reveal a clique fixated on self harming with a fine parochialism that could hardly have been better calculated to erode the confidence of financiers. Yet the talent truly is there, and over the last few years there has been so much to celebrate in Scottish film production that my impression is that our film-makers may now be finding it more rewarding to concentrate on production and to keep profitless bitching out of public print. Perhaps this is in part a consequence of the recruitment of the first waves of graduates from film and media studies programmes, a younger generation that has a more accurately tuned understanding of what they can expect if they work in the Scottish media.

Recent releases have included some outstanding productions. Yet despite its high reputation, I did not look forward to seeing Ken Loach's *Sweet Sixteen.* Although it seems not to have been widely recognised, British cinema of the past twenty years has exhibited a continuing fascination with the misery of working-class lives, to the extent that the accumulated films amount to a small sub-genre. Many of Loach's films have contributed to this body of work. I suggest that when we look back in a few years time a good part of this sub-genre will seem stifling and melodramatic. In some ways more interesting than the films themselves is the obsession of a cinema-going audience which has steadily been getting wealthier with the poverty portrayed unknown to most of them. This bizarre need is also fed by the colour supplements' routine juxtaposition of pages about, say, the agony of HIV/AIDS sufferers in Southern Africa with vivid photographs celebrating gourmet living and the most fashionable consumables to be found on the high street. I suspect it is a distinctive and specifically British cultural phenomenon to assuage the guilt of the educated middle-classes for their good fortune. As it happened, I found *Sweet Sixteen* one of Ken Loach's finest movies – better than most in the sub-genre. It is effective in tying the misery of its protagonists to a devastating social problem – the destruction that heroin wreaks on good lives. Loach's film made the pain almost tangible in the damage done to a likable boy whose life is destroyed by an involvement in the drug scene.

Morvern Callar captures wonderfully Alan Warner's young heroine whose boyfriend's seemingly motiveless suicide forces upon her a terrible awakening. To survive, she has to find a way, step by hesitant step, to cope with the devastation of her life. Playing Morvern, Samantha Morton embodies the young woman's confusion, her intuitive discovery of ways to handle her predicament and her eventual new-found confidence. Lynne Ramsay directs camera, pop music and dazzling editing to create a simulacrum of Morvern's evolving states of mind as she tries drink, drugs, sex, friendship, and, having disposed of the body, a little common sense larceny. She empties her boyfriend's bank account and uses the proceeds and the advance on the novel he has left her to sell and smashes her way out of the stifling existence of a supermarket shelf stacker.

What so impressed me about this stunning film is the energy with which Morvern embarks on a journey of self-discovery which she certainly would not have been able to conceive of as such before being forced into it. That and the growing and vivid cinematic exhilaration with which Ramsay and her crew have created the emergence of the heroic woman from the girl's previously unformed character, grooving as it had been in the hazy dreams of youth. In an unexpected way, *Morvern Callar* for me resembles another deeply absorbing film released at about the same time – *Donnie Darko* (Richard Kelly). In this film, the young hero Donnie succumbs to what, if you read the film at its obvious entry level, must be schizophrenia. There is an alternative interpretation of his trials in which he gains access to knowledge of the swift coiling of time, circumstance and precognition of a universe far removed from the Newtonian world of linear time and space governed in fiction by the certainties of cause and effect. Some such drowning in the vortex of her collapsing world could have been Morvern's fate as madness and despair rush in on her after her boyfriend's suicide. She survives and flourishes simply by trusting the health of her instincts. It is as if he had to die to cede her the space in which to make herself complete.

David Mackenzie's *Young Adam* succeeds exactly where his *The Last Great Wilderness* failed (that wilderness theme again!). The earlier film is an allegory for a time-branded cliché that periodically afflicts film production in Scotland. In this the

London-based sophisticate (perhaps a surrogate for the exiled film-maker) takes the road north to the never failing wildness of nature and the human heart. Mackenzie's film plays with those stereotypes, and to its credit varies the equally time-honoured stereotype of discovering the weird rustic natives to be not so much noble savages as noble savants. This film comes up with an energetic and satisfactorily nasty tale of self-discovery, but for all that, its weakness is that in the end it is what Dilys Powell used to call "a so-what film". You enjoy your time in the cinema, but when you go out onto the street at its end, nothing much is left in your head. This is because *The Last Great Wilderness* has adopted all too nakedly a no less familiar set of stereotypes. In taking us straight into a wilderness like T.S. Eliot's, where the soul of humankind is hellishly dark, it flags its themes with a time-worn symbolism that does not engage the enquiring mind.

The key to the success of *Young Adam* is the way that it sits brooding in the memory as an unusually dark film – notwithstanding it has a fair number of day-time exterior sequences. The darkness comes not only from Giles Nuttgens's camera work in realising the gloomy back street bars and tenements of the 1950s Clyde but also – this is indeed Scottish noir – from the relentless, grim repressions whose violations it plots. The story, based on Alexander Trocchi's novel, is simple but Mackenzie handles its thematic material with a subtlety that enhances the malaise surrounding his characters' emotionally parched lives.

In his mid thirties, Joe (Ewan McGregor) has drifted into work on a barge that shifts coal along the Clyde and Forth Canal. He and his boss Les (Peter Mullan) pull the body of a drowned girl from the water. Something about her sexuality in death fascinates them both, all the more so when the police bring a man to court charged with her murder. Les's morbid interest seems in a distorted way to reflect the decay of his own physical relationship with his wife Ella (Tilda Swinton). For Joe the fascination worms even deeper. Observing the sexual neediness of Ella, whom dull labours and Les's inert affection have driven into drudgery, Joe, whose one skill is seduction, becomes her lover. The sex is dangerous (and the more compelling for it) both because of their mutual ferocity and, as lust grips them, their disregard of the risk that Les will discover them. When he does, it seems as if Joe wanted to face the older man's anger; but when, rather than fight, Les quits the barge leaving Ella to him, the fire that fuels Joe's desire for her dwindles. Having given her back not only her sexuality but also her passion, he breaks with her brutishly by not troubling to conceal that he has casually fucked her brazen sister. In effect, Joe walks away from the love he has aroused in Ella, and soon enters listlessly on another, short-term sexual liaison with a woman who becomes his landlady.

Walking away from things is Joe's trade mark, for while all this is going on we discover via flashback sequences that the drowned woman, far from being unknown to him, was his lover Cathie (Emily Mortimer); but the story of their time together ekes out so fragmentarily that it appears to be something that Joe himself would rather not have to remember. Here was a girl who had loved him and kept him while he fiddled for months at the typewriter without writing anything. Eventually when neither good nor bad sex proved sufficient compensation for his emotional and spiritual inertia, she threw him out. But they meet again by chance after he has joined the barge and she tries to get him back by making love near the water's edge. When Joe as usual prepares to make his exit and turns his back on her, Cathie, erratic in her distress, falls off the dock and drowns accidentally. This is the corrosive knowledge that Joe has been carrying with him. Yet his inertia is not dissipated even when an innocent man is condemned to hang for her murder, although Joe knows there has been no killing. He fails to act decisively to rescue the other man; but walking away this time leaves him locked in a limbo mainly of his own making.

Young Adam is an intriguing title – one which implies that the film will take a moral stance. Joe is not strikingly young except in being ignorant of the debt he owes to the original sinner – so he is the new Adam, and a wretched disappointment at that, compared with the new man of Christian millennial anticipation. A character completely without morals, he stands out in high profile in the hypocritically moralistic ethos of the the film's 1950s. It's a device which makes Joe's projection to 2003 audiences more visible. For today he would surely not be that readily picked out among the legions of young and not-so-young men who (sanctioned by our society's rampant materialism) commit to nothing and act to suit only their own short-term appetites.

The outstanding cinema book recently published is *Dickens and the Dream of Cinema* (Manchester University Press, 2003). Its Scottish connection is all the more gratifying in that author Grahame Smith is a former colleague at the University of Stirling. He starts by examining the influence of Dickens and his age on the gestation of cinema; and then he reverses the lens to consider the impact of cinema and television on twentieth-century reworkings of the great writer. Enlivening the careful academic analysis, *Dickens and the Dream of Cinema* resonates with the exhilaration of a writer who has found the ideal theme to unify two of his life's passions – the Victorian novelist and the silver screen. What results is a wonderful book.

One of the many pleasures of this erudite work is that, in taking a fresh look at the issue of how to value the adaptations into new forms of primary texts, Smith rediscovers a number of theorists of art. Among them, he recovers Walter Benjamin. As Smith reads him, Benjamin makes a visionary case for the permeability of art forms. This perception buttresses André Bazin's thoughts on adaptation. The latter recognised that the reworking of pre-existing texts is so commonplace that the notion of the unity of a work of art can no longer be sustained. When a novel is adapted into say both a play and a film, what results is not a group of three works one of which is by definition better or more authentic than the other. Rather the three together make a single work which Bazin describes as "an artistic pyramid with three sides". Incidentally, the happy conjunction of Benjamin, Bazin and Smith on this theme makes for as persuasive a case as any I know for the true value of the multiple layering of post-modern texts – not just a play with aesthetics, but a compounding and enriching of meaning as well. Smith uses these insights into what he provocatively terms "the impurity of art" as the key to open the cultural past, present and future of Dickens's work

Firstly, paying due tribute to Sergei Eisenstein's famous essay concerning Dickens's impact on D.W. Griffith, Smith shows how the novelist's vision often preceded that of narrative cinema. The earlier epoch, as Walter Benjamin argued, can here be seen dreaming the period that was to follow. There is indeed much evidence to show that Dickens lived in an era which prepared the ground for cinema, with his own life's work doing much to augment the necessarily profound shift in popular perceptions of the world. This was partly a consequence of the speed and urgency of life in the new cities; but the new urban experience was itself enhanced by new, vivid and mind-engrossing ways of representing the busy streets. Through the early and mid nineteenth century a popular passion for moving vistas (amounting in effect to a new way of seeing) was aroused by immensely successful public exhibitions of magic lantern shows, phantasmagoria, panoramas and dioramas. All these developments were absorbed by Dickens.

In the second part of the book Smith discusses a number of adaptations for both the large and small screens of Dickens's novels. He critiques them according to the degree of their success in contributing to that overarching, multi-faceted artistic pyramid, the larger single work. With few exceptions, however, the challenge tends to have been too much for most of the adapters. David Lean's *Oliver Twist* is in Smith's judgment the most successful reworking.

The book ends fittingly with a dream epilogue in which Smith conjures the wraith of one of his heroes, Orson Welles, and celebrates the aesthetic and thematic links between the two authors' works. Not hard to sense here that, stirred by the triumph of Welles's *The Magnificent Ambersons*, Smith yearns for yet another film that the maverick American never quite made, seeing Welles as the perfect partner for Dickens.

And yearning is exactly what the medium does for me. At its oh-so-frequent best, the cinema leaves the enthusiast caught almost (but never wholly) fulfilled between exhilarated memories and impossible yearning for what the big screen may bring next. That's the happy posture in which at least one Scottish film-lover finds himself at the end of 2003.

Part V: Culture of Scotland

Art

Cordelia Oliver

It is twelve years or so since I ceased to be a working art critic, a professional regularly trawling the Scottish gallery scene for subjects worth discussion. But, and it is a sizeable but, I have been around the Scottish art scene for some six decades, as art student, painter, part-time commercial artist and – for more of these years than I care to remember – art critic for two serious newspapers. To begin with, in the late 1950s, I was invited to become the traditionally anonymous "Our Art Critic" – the first woman to hold the post, incidentally – for what was then the *Glasgow Herald.* And, within two years, my services had been invited to the *Times* and what was then the *Manchester Guardian.* Very briefly I juggled with both outlets, but before long the *Manchester Guardian* won the day – not least because, besides being my favourite journal, its then features editor was the unique Brian Redhead who promptly gave me my own byline and began to trust my judgment about what might be worth printing.

So I can boast a very long experience in the business of looking at artworks in the widest sense, listening to what artists – and would-be artists (for the two are by no means the same) – have had to say about their own work and that of their contemporaries, and attempting to put my own thoughts and opinions – the latter not always easily come by, incidentally – into a given number of printed words within a given time. My own art education has spanned the influence of two fine teachers: Hugh Adam Crawford, RSA, at Glasgow School of Art who was essentially broad-minded but by no means an easy-going master while James Cowie, RSA, during my summer at Hospitalfield, I found to be much narrower in his views on painting and painters. Both men, however, put drawing very high on the list of essentials. That, then, was my creative upbringing an art appreciation – that, and wide reading.

The fifties saw Scotland just beginning to be aware of abstraction, as such, almost entirely through reproduction. Scottish painting was mostly experienced by means of two major exhibitions, the Royal Scottish Academy in Edinburgh and the Royal Glasgow Institute. There was also a third annual exhibition, held in the RSA galleries, that of the Society of Scottish Artists to which young painters like myself in the later 1940s aimed to join as professional members. And it was the SSA which, by long tradition, offered invitations to notable foreign artists. One such was de Stael in the mid 1950s; and, in the 1970s, work by Romanian Paul Neagu had a powerful effect on young talent.

Edinburgh and Glasgow – Aberdeen also — had always had fine public galleries where budding artists might feed on works which presented a blend of craft and imagination. In the private sector Edinburgh had Aitken Dott's Scottish Gallery which offered solo exhibitions to both senior and up-and-coming Scottish artists – by and large, it has to be said, putting most emphasis on Edinburgh-based talent; Gillies and Mactaggart-the-younger, for example, with Redpath, Philipson and their juniors Blackadder and Houston. My own opinion remains that, apart from Gillies (who went his own delightful way, regardless), this absolute certainty of local acceptance was not always good for true development in every case. The obvious exception was Joan Eardley for whom Aitken Dott's was originally the main outlet where her little off-the-cuff sketches of Glasgow slum children were both welcome and energetically promoted. But Eardley's vision could not so easily be corralled. Her discovery of the North sea coast at Catterline led to the wonderfully energetic canvasses which proved – at least to begin with – much less easy to sell.

Glasgow's once rich private gallery scene had fallen away before and after the Second World War. The city's resurgence as a centre of contemporary art depended to some extent on the presence, not just of Polish immigrants like Josef Herman but also of J.D. Fergusson and his influence on the New Art Club. Energy began to rise again in 1964, when some local artists, notably Tom MacDonald, Bet Low and John Taylor, tired of hanging their work on park railings, opened the New Charing Cross Gallery in an attic above an art materials shop in Sauchiehall Street. Its success, and its almost inevitable closure after three or four years, led one of its directors, Cyril Gerber, to open his Compass Gallery nearby where much up-and-coming talent has had its first serious showing. That was in March 1969, since when the whole scene in Scotland, Glasgow not least, has erupted. Small galleries now abound, commercial enterprises along with Scottish Arts Council-funded WASPS as well as print and sculpture studios in all the main connurbations and small towns alike. In one sense, for someone looking back, the openings for budding artists have seldom been so good. Commerce, indeed, has never been more promotional, with all kinds of art-making, professional and amateur, catered for in the most unlikely shops. And that must be welcomed even when it leads to signs announcing “Make your Own Art”.

But – and here is a sizeable but – in a period like ours, on the cusp of a century cross-over, certainties seem more than ever out of the question, not least for octogenarians like me. I have lived through the surge of so-called conceptual art without any problem – Joseph Beuys and Tadyeus Kantor, to name just two important examples brought to Britain in the 1970s by the indefatigable Richard Demarco, were obviously powerful and influential artists both in vision and creative intelligence (hands-on as well as intellectual) and both, as it happens, were extremely fine draughtsmen. Earlier, indeed, as an art student through the forties, I “came in” so to say, with Picasso, Matisse and the later American abstractionists. But that was a time when pupils, who, like me, happened to be to some extent gifted both creatively and intellectually, would be pressurised at school into a university career.

I was fortunate: my father – a marine engineer who, himself, had managed to thwart his own parents’ desire to make him a lawyer – saw no problem in letting me study painting at Glasgow School of Art instead of history and English at Glasgow University. I still have a letter from my former English teacher written long after her retirement, in which, having read some of my reviews in the *Manchester Guardian*, she declared herself delighted to see that I was now "exercising my brain and expressing myself succinctly and well." What she thought I had been doing all these years at Art School and after, I cannot imagine.

Why, you may ask, have I digressed into my autobiography. I will tell you. For the last two decades at least, the schools of art in Scotland, following the English example, began to award BA degrees in place of the former diploma, thus attracting grammar school pupils who are more "clever" than truly creative and who find a now fashionable career in the visual arts very attractive – potentially lucrative also, as was seldom the case in the old days. Popular photography, the cinema, TV and video and evermore blatant advertising – all these have had an effect on the work of art students. Computers, even more so, have seen a reduction in what I remain convinced is an absolute essential for budding artists of any kind, the need to draw. Eventually, of course, the way all these developments have fed into the visual arts of our time will surely begin to seem not just natural but absolutely right – but only in the best work. For it is important to remember that a tiny percentage of art work done at any one time is going to be good enough to take seriously and, what is more, to last. It is also important to realise that even a great artist can have his low points. The recent *Monet and the Sea* exhibition during the 2003 Edinburgh Festival was a great disappointment in that much of the work on display was far below the painter's best. That is what tends to happen when the selection is entrusted to so-called art scholars.

What I am trying to say is that increasingly "ideas" have tended to take over visual arts, and the Turner Prize raises "ideas art" to a status which, for me, it does not deserve. When at Tramway in his early years, Douglas Gordon offered a vision of the powerful Hitchcock film *Psycho*, slowed down to twenty-four hours in length (very few people watched it for more than a few minutes) or when another artist covered the floor of a large gallery in the new Dundee Contemporary Arts centre with polystyrene bricks declaiming a succession of vulgarisms, both were treated far more seriously than their offerings deserved. More visually impressive by far (and that is what matters after all) was the earlier event staged by one of the best Dundee-trained artists, David Mach, who, by stacking magazines tightly round the slender columns of Tramway 2, caused a magical transformation, giving the vast space the appearance of an ancient Egyptian temple. Sometimes it seems as though scale is all: yet the real power of Jim Lambie's eye-dazzling striped floors comes nowhere near the optical magic generated by Bridget Riley in wall-hung prints. But no: I am far from complaining about artists who have turned their back on painting and sculpture as such. Patricia MacDonald, who has aimed her camera on areas of Scotland from her husband's aeroplane, has managed to produce a series of wonderful colour photographs which could easily hold their own against any fine paintings, so exciting are they in composition and atmospheric quality and currently, as I write, the teamwork of Mathew Dalziel and Louise Scullion are transforming the ground floor space in Glasgow's Gallery of Modern Art with a multi-media exhibition, *Storm,* which, in projected images and commentary, aims to explore the sheer unrelenting energy of nature.

Too often, however, so-called conceptualism has, more than almost any other form, taken hold of "ideas art" and produced far too much pedestrian work. Yet, in the footsteps of Beuys and Kantor, we have had rich and meaningful offerings by award-winning local artists, notably Kate Whiteford's grass sculpture on Calton Hill, and even more meaningful, George Wyllie's Straw Locomotive which hung, high above the Clyde, from the great Finnieston Crane, for the whole summer in that same year, 1988. Wyllie, like me in his eighties, remains hard at work in the west of Scotland, but the much younger Whiteford has found it necessary to go south.

Painters, too, carry on regardless – the galleries are full of colourful still lifes, mostly flowers and fruit, attempting to follow the now so fashionable "Scottish Colourists". And in the wake of the heavily promoted "New Glasgow Boys" during the 1980s, figurative painting, too, is back in fashion. The two Johns, Bellany and Byrne (the latter also talented as a playwright), top the list in that respect, since of the younger set, only Ken Currie has begun to find his true fulfilment. Among older women painters Lys Hansen's formidable contribution can never be overlooked. And what a pity that the work of Margot Sandeman – still, with the late Joan Eardley, first among my own contemporaries – is seldom if ever seen in public galleries. The occasional maverick – I think of Ian Hamilton Finlay – a political concrete *poet au fond* – can even rise to fame beyond Scotland by teaming up with (some would say making use of) talented visual artists. What is far more rare is to find high visual creativity linked in a single individual with great diplomacy and organising ability. I can think of only one outstanding example, that of the fine painter, Ian McKenzie Smith who, during his term as Director, raised Aberdeen Art Gallery to a level unusual in any such provincial institution, and is now masterminding as its President, the far from usual developments in the Royal Scottish Academy.

Scotland's visual arts scene is, then, lively as never before. In this new century (forget about the millennium) the means of making art have changed and expanded beyond what any art student of my generation could possibly have envisaged. But beware the notion that art is what you think it is, and that anyone can be an artist who so wishes. What is true is that any individual possessed by the true creative urge, and the will to work in order to express it fully, has been born in the right period.

Part V: Culture of Scotland

Theatre

Gail MacDonald

To be or not to be? That has been the question since February 1922 when the Scottish National Theatre Society was formed. Its aims were to develop Scottish drama, to encourage the public's taste for good plays and to found a National Theatre. At last, after many false starts, the dream is now closer to reality. The Scottish Executive has announced a £37.5 million funding package to establish the foundations, appoint an artistic director and a small administration staff. The finance minister Andy Kerr has said: "We believe that culture and the arts have a key role in today's diverse Scotland. Our vision is for a Scotland where our cultural life is inclusive and accessible." The fact is that culture and the arts have always played a key role; it has just taken this long for the people in charge to realise it. It is the news the theatre community and indeed the community in general have been waiting for, but which for many has also underlined the seriousness of the project. The focus now has to turn towards how we can make it work.

The model for the project is not one of expensive buildings that keep going over budget and over schedule. Instead, the Scottish National Theatre will be essentially a commissioning and performance body, recruiting the skills of existing theatre companies for productions that will tour the country. The artistic director will either commission new work, extend the run of exceptional plays produced by these companies, or fund revivals of productions which see only one run. There will be small-scale and large-scale productions, plays for adults and plays for children, work with and for schools and constructive partnerships with youth and community theatre. Instead of sucking energies and money inward to sustain its structures, the National Theatre will look outwards to engage theatre artists and audiences in a truly national venture. Without the bureaucracy, which has the potential to bring the project to its knees, the Scottish National Theatre should be able to concentrate on lifting theatrical standards up where they belong.

Proposals for a National Theatre have spent years in the wings, with an expectant theatre community and audiences awaiting their entry. It has been emblematic of much of the debate about Scotland's identity and how, in a devolved Scotland, the arts can best contribute to our society and its cultural identity. But by and large, we don't regard theatre as very important. There's a general muttering every time the subject comes up that theatre is too elitist, too expensive, too highbrow, and that it fails to connect with a wide audience. Yet theatre is actually becoming more accessible to a wide-ranging cross section of the population. The fears of not knowing where to go and what to wear are dissipating fast; dress codes are being relaxed and falling ticket prices are enticing a more "normal" audience to see shows. The fact remains, however, that no matter how accessible theatre becomes, and no matter how excited we become about the prospect of a National Theatre, the Scottish Parliament dedicates less than a quarter of one per cent of its annual budget to culture. Quite frankly, it is a miracle we have any artistic activity at all in Scotland.

The arts provide the most democratic success of any endeavour. Anyone from any background can succeed; money and privilege can never buy creativity. But in Scotland we don't yet have the confidence to place the arts at the centre of our culture and economy. The hostility towards the subsidised arts is countered only with persistence and by providing the examples of other countries where culture and the arts are calculable parts of economic development, such as the Netherlands. The arts in Scotland are an integral part of the economy, contributing £5 billion and 70,000 jobs, but more needs to be done to strengthen and sustain this. The arts can help us re-make our place in the world and maintain Scotland as a great place to live and visit. If there is one service that the arts can provide, let it be that. A National Theatre can help us see new horizons and lend courage to new ambitions. It is the chance to present the bigger picture and show how the arts can work for Scotland.

The National Theatre project has the potential to create a meeting point for education, theatre, Scottish festivals and all the creative industries. It is vital that children are given the opportunity to express themselves through the arts as individuals and realise their potential. Participation in the arts, particularly for young people, can be a life-changing experience. A drama workshop, a writer in residence, holding a musical instrument for the first time, any of these can be a liberating and determining moment in a person's life.

We must ensure, therefore, that young people have open access to the arts and that their experience is of the highest possible quality. The National Theatre cannot shy away from its educational duties. Every Scottish school, college and university has to have access to it. The young boy or girl who is now sitting in a classroom somewhere in Scotland is the young man or woman who will eventually perform in theatres throughout Scotland and who will help build the theatre community throughout the country. Children and young people are central to the National Theatre. The Executive has pledged more than £3 million for schools' cultural co-ordinators, focused on developing and nurturing the talent of young people. To bring theatre to children is to bring them a great gift. Access to good-quality theatre is a resource we have a duty to provide just as much as books or lighting equipment or lesson plans. Izzy Swanson, a drama co-ordinator for Shetland Islands Council, said: "I hope that a National Theatre will have an education unit and will be keen to get out and about. Education sometimes gets shrugged off as the 'b' team, but that needn't and shouldn't be the case."

The National Theatre is an investment in learning. The new organisation will be in pole position to represent theatre in the world of education, to support drama teachers across the country, and to deliver touring work for schools. The job of the National Theatre will not be to replace the good work already being done in education, by the Scottish Youth Theatre for example, but to support, widen and integrate the interface with schools.

But what about the people who who are going to make this venture a success? No one can doubt the abilities of our actors, writers, directors, producers, designers and technicians. These skills need to be nurtured, affirmed and profiled. Perhaps we cannot claim a finished or polished dramatic tradition, but we have something else, the raw materials to forge something new for the future. Scotland has a rich dramatic history of conflict, a verbal energy and a strong sense of live occasion. We also have an outward-looking capacity to harness the best in world theatre and to speak on the international stage in our own distinctive accents. Yet, as distinctive as they might be, these accents have, in recent years, been forced out of Scotland by the current funding climate. The author Janice Galloway, the theatre director Kenny Ireland and the Scottish Arts Council chairman, James Boyle, have all expressed their concerns that a lack of commitment to theatre in Scotland is driving away the nation's finest talent.

Theatre in Scotland has been chronically under-funded for almost a decade. Individual theatres have suffered from local authority cutbacks and touring companies have seen the pot of available funding dwindle over the years. Amazing, then, that in the midst of this, the industry can still push talent through. Robbie Coltrane, Robert Carlisle and Shirley Henderson all performed in Scottish theatre before moving onto the big and small screen. *Trainspotting* only became a film hit after it was first staged at the Citizens Theatre in Glasgow. But the danger is that the talent simply passes through and moves on to better places.

This may have a lot to do with the most recent funding budget announced by the Scottish Arts Council. The increase in budget is less than the rate of inflation, which represents a cut in funds in real terms for many arts organisations. By January this year, funding difficulties were so acute that the £1 million set aside by the SAC for the National Theatre project was assigned instead to bolstering the regional companies. A spokeswoman for the Executive said: "The Executive has recognised concerns expressed with Scottish theatre infrastructure and the additional funds are being allocated to strengthen that infrastructure and to put the Scottish theatre on a firm footing for the future." James Boyle, Chairman of the SAC, said: "The extra money we have recently invested in strengthening Scottish theatre across the board has helped raise audience levels and increase confidence among the profession. The time is now right to build on Scottish talent and skills by establishing the National Theatre of Scotland."

Unless funding equivalent to that available in England and Wales is made available here, there will still be a drift of talent southward that will result in the ability of professional theatre to survive in Scotland being undermined. Provincial theatres in England benefited from a £25 million funding package in 1999, while theatres such as Dundee Rep, the Traverse and the Royal Lyceum operate on publicly funded budgets of under £1 million, less than half of that awarded to equivalents in England such as Manchester's Royal Exchange Theatre or the West Yorkshire Playhouse in Leeds. The English now spend more per head on theatre than their counterparts in this country.

Dr Donald Smith, who chaired the steering group for the National Theatre, categorically stated: "If the Executive is serious about presenting Scottish culture, it needs a champion like a National Theatre." But is it serious? Gordon MacLean of An Tobar Theatre Company in Mull, says of the Executive's funding strategy: "Let's not let the Scottish Executive think they're off the hook because they've given the arts £7 million, which was a tiny bit of their unspent budget. That's the kind of money they use to re-carpet their offices. The Scottish Arts Council is still hugely under-funded and the fabulous resource which is the Scottish arts scene is still undervalued and full of committed people working for buttons."

Around Scotland, the Executive is pursuing a strategy which demands access to the arts in all the towns and cities: a strategy undoubtedly to be praised but also impossible to deliver in the current funding climate. When Inverness missed out on the bid to become the European Capital of Culture in 2008, Jack McConnell, the First Minister, announced that 2006 would be the Scottish Year of Highland Culture – except that 2006 (like our Parliament building, the years just keep on being added), has turned into 2007 and who's to say when the Highlands will ever celebrate its year of culture, and whether the infrastructure will be there to support it.

The main issue that the Executive continues to dodge is not the sum available to theatre but the core amounts required by each theatre company and arts development organisations to function properly. The Stockholm City Theatre receives an annual allowance of £22 million. That is nearly three times the initial funding allocated for the National Theatre project; seven times the size of the annual grant requested by the steering committee to support the project; eighteen times the size of the annual sum actually allocated by the Executive to build up Scotland's theatre infrastructure in advance of that project. Either Scotland wants a world-class theatre and pays for it, or it does not. We have long been calling out for decent funding of the arts and now that some commitment is being shown to a National Theatre, we must make sure it does not take away from any of the existing theatre companies, some of which are still struggling to survive. What of them in the new, national climate?

The creation of a National Theatre should mean that the potential of Scottish theatre can be realised and the focus can be raised internationally, as should the potential for attracting more money into the sector in general. Jeremy Raison, of the Citizens Theatre, said the new theatre must not drain existing resources: "If you can raise the profile of Scottish theatre internationally, that's great. If you can take more work around all of Scotland, that's great. It shouldn't be seen, though, as a complete panacea, we still have funding problems here, as do many theatres." If these theatres continue to have funding problems while the National Theatre goes from strength to strength, that in turn will become another problem. Jack McConnell, however, insists this will not happen. He has said that the National Theatre will not be formed at the expense of regional theatre, but that instead it will build on Scotland's regional theatre.

The nerve centre for the National Theatre will be a housing estate in Glasgow once blighted by drugs and violence. The Executive believes that its decision to site the headquarters in Easterhouse shows a commitment to bringing theatre to disadvantaged communities, an admirable but nevertheless brave move. The Easterhouse Arts Factory is part of a £9.3 million development, which includes a swimming pool, a further education college, performance space, a library, rehearsal rooms, darkrooms and a centre for lifelong learning. Due for completion in 2005 (we hold our breath), it has received funding from European bodies and the National Lottery. It's a pioneering example of bringing theatre to the masses. The arts allow people to rise above the purely materialistic and appreciate there is more to life than goods and gain. Frank McAveety, Minister for Culture, said when announcing the site for the administrative headquarters: "The responsibility of the National Theatre will be towards the people of Scotland; it is their theatre. It is about making the arts relevant to our communities and the people who live there. It is therefore fitting that Easterhouse, which has demonstrated a commitment to the arts as part of the area's regeneration, should be our preferred location."

So, against all odds, theatre in Scotland is starting to flourish again. As the *Guardian* put it: "Last week, two announcements were made about national theatres. One was in Edinburgh, the other in New York. One was radical and forward-looking, the other tired and old-fashioned. Curiously, it is little old Scotland, not New York, where the agenda is being set."

Now the onus is on us. Scotland certainly has the talent, the history and the voice to be creative. Do we have the commitment? The National Theatre must plan its first season carefully in a way that stretches as well as entertains audiences, attracts attention and stimulates our writers, directors and designers. It should be fun, exciting, glamorous, stimulating, moving but never pretentious. It should be an inclusive, educational, wide-ranging, all-encompassing vehicle of which Scotland can be proud.

The answer to the question was always "to be"; but to be good, we cannot afford mistakes.

Part V: Culture of Scotland

Poetry

Tessa Ransford

A conference at the Arches in Glasgow was run recently by a group from London called Artists in Exile. People were invited to ask questions or say what they most wished for if such a group were to be formed in Glasgow. One English girl asked if she belonged, since she wasn't in exile. Then she added: "But all artists feel like exiles in society." She was right, and I applauded in my heart. The poet, in particular, is regarded as either a fool or an angel.

It is hard to tell anyone that you are a poet. Overcoming this has been one of the many campaigns I have waged over the last twenty years through the Scottish Poetry Library. I suggested we called ourselves "practising poets", in as much as we practise the art rather than theorise about it; we keep on practising all our lives; we practise it in the community too in a variety of ways, if we are allowed. Most poets nowadays make what income they can from running workshops, holding residencies, helping others – often with more of a social and therapeutic than of an aesthetic aim or outcome. The two are not exclusive, but the interest of the funder is usually the social outcome. If all this activity to help others to write poetry were to be successful it would only result in more scarcely-published poets looking for work running workshops.

After being excluded from an academic book about Scottish women poets of the last quarter century, I was relieved to find I was included in a recent Canongate anthology of twentieth-century women poets. At the launch, I told of a conversation I had had twenty years earlier with Sandy Moffat, the artist who painted the now famous portrait of seven poets in Milnes Bar: MacDiarmid,

MacCaig, Goodsir Smith, Garioch, Mackay Brown, Crichton Smith and Morgan. I had asked him, "When are you going to paint seven women poets?" "Are there?" he replied. I told him I could name twenty off the top of my head. We went on in the Scottish Poetry Library to exhibit, list, catalogue, computerise, make visible and available in every way we could the women poets past and present of Scotland, in whatever language, as we did with various other groupings under which poets can be gathered and sought.

I'm not worried about being a woman poet. I know I'm a woman and am happy to be one. As a poet I'm not choosing my gender but my metier. I'm not trying to be Scottish in my poetry either, though Scotland is my home and inevitably in my poetry since it is in my daily consciousness and culture. It has been my home since I was ten years old. It is hard for people to cope when they don't quite know how to categorise you. Yes, a poet, but a woman; yes, Scottish but not born in Scotland or with a marked Scottish accent; yes, intellectual but not an academic; yes, passionate but not political; yes, poor but not working-class.

Colin Bell, one-time radio presenter, met me at the Wigtown Festival the other day where he was reading from a murder novel he has written; the reading had been well-attended, he was pleased to tell me. He, and all the other main speakers were about to leave, it being Sunday afternoon at the end of the festival's three days. I was scheduled for 4pm on that Sunday, to read my translations of poets from former East Germany, well-known over Eastern Europe but not previously translated into English. I told Colin I was afraid I might not have much of an audience. "Well Tessa," he said, "you're an ascetic." I think he meant "aesthetic" but perhaps not? I went away wondering what he did mean. Perhaps he meant I was a poet, and as such in his view rather intellectual and therefore probably not a sensual woman? I had an attentive and appreciative audience of about twenty people from Wigtown and Galloway, including John Pick, the excellent poet and biographer of Neil Gunn with his wise wife, both of them old, who had made a long drive over to hear me.

I considered myself to have had a run of luck in being included in the anthology and to have been invited to read at Wigtown. The

German translations have at last found a small publisher in Devon keen to publish them, if he can find a grant or sponsorship. The book would include photographs and drawings of the poets and an academic appreciation of their work from an Oxford specialist in that field. No Scottish publisher was interested. The Scottish Arts Council can't give a grant to an English publisher, so I cannot count on the book coming to pass. Similarly the Edinburgh International Book Festival cannot invite some of the East Germans to read next year unless they can find sponsorship specifically for this "esoteric" event. I was able to go to Leipzig in 2002 to meet and translate the poets thanks to a travelling scholarship from the Society of Authors, based in London, for which I was nominated by Trevor Royle, then serving on that committee for the Society as a Scottish representative. The artist, Joyce Gunn Cairns, came with me on an SAC grant to draw and photograph the poets. Yet when we returned with the drawings, photographs and translations no one wanted to sponsor an exhibition or publication. The organisation Arts and Business failed us dismally. The German Consulate couldn't suggest any firm to approach. The City of Edinburgh couldn't help. The Book Festival couldn't help. The National Portrait Gallery couldn't help. We gave up the idea of an exhibition with readings and instead I paid for a CD to be made of the images, for a power-point presentation, something I only recently learned was possible.

Strangely enough it is easier psychologically to struggle to find a publisher for translations of East Germans than for my own poems. For them I have turned to pamphlets and the tried and trusted expertise of Duncan Glen's Akros publications. In 1998, reaching sixty and with seven books and two early pamphlets behind me, I realised that I would not be able to find a publisher for my *Selected Poems*. The publisher would need a grant and that would not be forthcoming from the SAC, judging from their having turned down a grant for my 1998 volume. Rather than have a thick volume published, with or without a grant, expensive, heavy, not likely to sell, I thought I would scatter my selected poems like petals from the rose in a series of themed pamphlets. Akros have published four so far: *Scottish Selection*, *Indian Selection*, *Natural*

Selection and *Noteworthy Selection* (the last being accompanied by notes on the poems by me). They cost very little; they weigh very little; they can be sold on the internet and never darken the doors of a chain bookshop. They will not be noticed or reviewed, given large literary prizes or recognised as adding to the world of literature.

My second husband died in 1999. He was Callum Macdonald from Bernera, Lewis, who built up a sizeable printing firm, Macdonald's Loanhead, and on the side published *Lines Review* poetry magazine from 1952-98 (144 issues) as well as some hundred books, two-thirds of them poetry. He asked me to edit *Lines Review* in 1988, which I continued to do for the next ten years. He was the main publisher for Robert Garioch and for Derick Thomson as well as for Iain Crichton Smith, later taken over by Carcanet in Manchester.

After Callum died, his printing firm was bought into by a bigger firm from Yorkshire and then suddenly closed down, putting some seventy people out of work. The chairman of the trustees asked me if I could think of a way of commemorating the firm and Callum. He said "We have £300 and a silver quaich used for staff golf tournaments." It took me twenty-four hours to think of setting up an annual award for the publisher of a poetry pamphlet.

Thanks to wonderful support from the National Library of Scotland and sponsorship from the Michael Marks Charitable Trust we set up the Callum Macdonald Memorial Award for the publishing of poetry in pamphlet form. The first award was in 2001 and the fourth will be in May 2004. The award has been surprisingly successful, with more and better quality pamphlets submitted each year and now its own website selling pamphlets online. We also instituted an annual Christmas fair and party where poetry pamphlets are bought and sold over mulled wine and mince pies. Pamphlet poets have given readings three times at the Edinburgh Book Festival (under the heading of "the writing business" sponsored by the Society of Authors), twice at the Radical Book Fair and once at a conference in Pitlochry of the Institute of Contemporary Scotland. We have recently made a video *Pamphlet Power, Poet Power* giving advice, encouragement and rationale for the making of pamphlets for poetry today. That, too, is available to buy online: www.scottish-pamphlet-poetry.com.

Leonard Wolfe, husband of Virginia, himself a publisher and fine-press printer, extolled the virtues of pamphlets: "The pamphlet is an extraordinarily good literary form from both the artistic and the social or political point of view." How can a poetry pamphlet be political? It is political by its very existence, independent of Arts Council control or of enslavement to the commercial world of bookselling. The internet provides an alternative route to reaching the interested public and the computer provides the technology for cheap, well-made, self-made *objets d'art*, combining poetry and production in an aesthetically pleasing ensemble.

Pamphlets for poetry provide the variety and quick turnaround that poetry needs. For too long it has not been understood on a par with other art forms such as painting or music, where a range of varieties is acknowledged within the genres. You can opt for classical, jazz or folk music as and when you choose. You can prefer conceptual or figurative art, oil painting or water-colour, but with poetry it seems people want only two categories: good or bad and that must depend on the judgment of Faber and Faber.

There seems to be an inordinate dread of "bad" poetry "overwhelming us". We are constantly overwhelmed by bad novels and bad writing of all kinds yet we manage to discriminate sufficiently to choose what we want to read. It is not often the case that what one generation considers "good" is also the choice of the next generation, and we should allow a sufficient variety to be published so that differences of taste and judgment can flourish in the future. By variety, I mean a variety of author and of kind of poetry. Like music, poetry is made in a range of kinds from haiku to epic with much in between. At present many good poets are not being published at all or very scantily. Most books of poetry, which are those published with public subsidy, go out of print or are remaindered within a couple of years, or less. Few are bought by libraries and very few see the shelves of bookshops. Those that do so are usually anthologies rather than an individual author's books and are from the well-known poetry publishers: Faber, Cape, Carcanet, Bloodaxe, Penguin. All poetry publications are subsidised, usually by arts councils. Naturally there is a limit to subsidy and it tends to go to the tried and trusted publishers and to poets who have already received grants, awards and fellowships from the same funding source. However benign or well-meaning the bureaucrats and their chosen committees of advisers, it is clear that this is an exclusive and prohibitive set-up.

It is for some of these reasons that I am now advocating pamphlets as the publication of choice for serious poets who want to make their way in the world, rather than in the Arts Council. Modern poetry, like modern art, can be devoid of meaning in the normal sense. This makes it beyond the comprehension of most of us but a charming game for those involved in it. It doesn't mean we should avoid it. The way it is written will probably be as clear as day to future generations, just as computer and video technology is to our primary school children now. But there are still many poets who believe that meaning matters and who try to convey it through the art form of poetry, using perhaps symbolism, metaphor, word-play, puns, refrains, allusions, metre, sound, patterns, verses.

I used to ask children in schools how they would decide a name for a dog. Naming would involve observation, allusion, sound, rhythm, appropriateness: the same elements as any poem. Human beings, having language, are naturally poetic. It is the way we think until we are maybe "schooled" out of it. For instance, I took my two-year old grandson to the swan and duck pond below Arthur's Seat recently, and on the way home he picked up a willowy piece of stick and bent it round, saying "look Granny, swan". He had captured the essence of swanness and reproduced it in a stick quite naturally. We are all too often schooled to be afraid of thinking this way or embarrassed by it. This is still the case in education though we should have left all that behind by now with the belt (and braces). However teachers, even in primary schools, avoid poetry now, for fear of putting the pupils off!

Verses are turns in the dance. Poetry is based on dance patterns. It is measured in feet, the ones at the end of our legs. It is phrased according to our gestures, heart-beat and breathing. It comes from the human form and from human life, encapsulating human mindfulness, intellect and emotion. In eastern and middle-eastern countries there is far less embarrassment about poetry than there is in Scotland or in Northern Europe. Here people will talk about it (sometimes), but begin to read or speak some and, unless you are in the pub with the excuse of drink, people will be mighty embarrassed. Even at the seemingly informal local ceilidh it is hard to interrupt the music and song with a poem, and takes some "neck" to say the least. In universities it is only the poets on the syllabus, whom the staff have studied and applied their latest theories to, who are acceptable. Some universities give posts to writers in residence as a resource for any students who might actually be doing some creative writing themselves.

There was no such resource when I was a student at Edinburgh University in the fifties. George Mackay Brown was also a student. *Lines Review* was being published. I never knew. I was writing poetry continuously from the age of six, and it never occurred to me that other people didn't. But I seem to have realised it wasn't something you mentioned. It was so much part of me however, that when I was beginning to embark on relationships with young men, I felt it important to confess to writing poetry. It was an instant turn-off! Eventually the poet settles for keeping quiet about it. I did that for years and years. When I did begin to publish some poems in the seventies I would be asked by kindly friends "How can you have time to write poetry when you have four children?" This used to make me feel guilty. Were they neglected? I lay awake at night wondering how I could deal with this. Then I decided my reply would be, "I don't bake and I don't knit" (neither of which was entirely true).

Even now, I find few friends who want to know about me as a poet. I spent a weekend at the cottage of one, with my daughter and grand-children. My daughter and I were looking at the new Canongate anthology of *20th Century Scottish Women Poets*, mentioned above, and discussing which poem I should read at the launch. It never occurred to our host over the weekend to pick up the book, or even ask me which of my poems were included. Similarly, I have been attached to the Centre for Human Ecology now for two and a half years as Royal Literary Fund Writing Fellow. I help students with their essays and also look at any creative writing they may be doing. I have also been tutoring a module called "Creativity in Life and Art". I have not been asked to give a reading of my own poems. This may be due to the fact that there are not funds to pay me, but as writing fellow I would not have required a fee. I have twice accompanied staff and students on the annual "fieldtrip" to the Isle of Eigg. There I have given a seminar on Gaelic poetry, showing the video of the film *Hallaig* about the life and poetry of Sorley MacLean based on his poem of the same name. The effect on the students and staff is intense, and leads to an opening up and a situation where it's now all right to talk about and read some poetry, their own and others.

These things are not so much disregarded in university circles as simply crowded out by the pressure on the timetable and syllabus of other more seemingly useful and necessary matters. But there is also a collective-unconscious fear and embarrassment about "creativity", partly because it cannot be put into the straitjackets of either morality or utility. We are back to the beginning again about poetry being on the margin – which is also "the edge" of course – and something really only for fools and angels. I would prefer it to be thought of as in the middle, the middle road taken by Thomas the Rhymer with the *Fairy Queen*, the balancing point between the desirable and the advisable. When it does become too established, with university courses set up to process poets for publication, or to give qualifications in creative writing, there is the danger of its "entering the castle."

To become an accepted contributor to the everyday life of society, however, is not the same as becoming too establishment. I was hearing complaints from Canongate about the cost of permissions from publishers for the poems in their women's anthology. I asked whether they would feel that way if they were paying for photographs? A surprised admission – "Well – no." Of course photographs have to be paid for, as does music, architecture, paintings, other forms of writing. Other artists try to live by their work; poets are not expected to do so. I am in favour of commissioned poetry, since I consider that any practising poet should be sufficiently professional to be able to write a good poem on any given theme.

My main aim in setting up and running the Scottish Poetry

Library was always to initiate ways of integrating poetry into the normal, everyday life of the people of Scotland again. The work we did in the Library, the cataloguing and lending, the events and exhibitions, projects and collaborations, were all designed to further the work of the Library, setting up branches, school visits, touring, networking and advising, making international and interarts links, creating a "field" in which poetry could grow and flourish. And the Library itself was to be welcoming, a place you could talk, breast-feed your baby, read, write, get help freely, confess to your addiction to poetry (a common theme), do research or find something your granny used to quote to you.

Now, as recently-elected President of Scottish PEN, I am on the same spiral but a different track. I am hoping to initiate projects that will help to integrate the many nationalities of writers in Scotland today, furthering and encouraging translation and a non-competitive ethos between writers, as well as fostering exchanges between Scottish writers and those from PEN centres abroad. I also want to go on caring for and presenting, wherever and whenever possible, the literature of Scotland past and present, with its trail of culture and history, work, philosophy, travel and invention.

We need not apologise for caring about our own culture. Only in so doing can we be in a position to take an interest in and relate to that of others. That is why I am deeply unhappy that we have no poetry programme on radio (or television) in Scotland and why I am tired of feeling an exile in respect of what matters most to me, my life as a poet, in the country which is my home.

I'd like more poetry to be accepted as the norm, for payment to poets to be accepted as the norm, for less embarrassment about what is natural and normal for human beings – to think and speak and write poetically, for the democratic intellect to find one way to fulfilment in the often painful integration of beauty with truth that becomes a poem of quality.

Part V: Culture of Scotland

Sport

Jim Delahunt

Back in August 1974, some thirty years ago now, a young boy trudged home from school across a sports field which the day before had hosted the trials for the St Andrews Academy under-thirteen football side in Saltcoats, Ayrshire. He was distraught, his world seemingly at an end. Stretched out ahead in his mind was the prospect of a whole season without playing football, the game which had become a religion as he'd practised morning, noon and night for the past eight years, firstly as a four-year-old in the street outside his house, then in interminable matches at the local park and on the concrete playground of his primary school where he'd eventually made the first XI in Primary Seven and collected two winners' medals. Everyone had known it was going to be tougher making the secondary school team as there were four primary schools streaming into the academy, fifty-odd first team players looking to make a sixteen-strong squad at the "big school". The standard was always going to be tough but the kid who wandered home in tears that night, making pacts with God about sacrifices to be made later on if only the decision to leave him out could be reversed, had only one crumb of consolation. There was to be a second trial in October and he was determined to prove the principal physical education teacher wrong.

I did. Life was back on track and worth living again. I also hoped that God would wait a few years before claiming the right arm I'd promised him two months before. Studies could now be tackled in the full knowledge that the real business of football was back on the agenda and for the next six years, barring nearly a year out with a knee problem, I would train five days a week, play two games on a

Saturday and a third on the Sunday, not to mention sundry friendlies and cup replays on Wednesday nights. My football career would not stretch beyond the Ayrshire amateur leagues but I lived for the game and, when I think back, would probably have died for it as well. An offer to join the rugby team instead had been viewed as simply abhorrent: in that school, the lads who played rugby were either deemed to be hopeless at football or of questionable sexual orientation. It was football or nothing.

Three decades on, thousands of kids in Scotland have the same attitude as I had towards the game. Many more can't live without rugby, golf, boxing, athletics, horse-riding, basketball, judo, karate and, where they can, tennis. Sadly, though, many thousands more get their daily sporting fix from twenty-four hour satellite coverage on Sky Sports, or from the more elaborate games they play on their home computers. Playing on the streets gave kids natural fitness which could be honed by coaching. In this electronic age, I'd wager that a huge percentage of our children couldn't run to the corner shop without getting out of breath.

While the occasional burst of brilliance from a Darren Fletcher (football), Simon Taylor (rugby union), Alastair Forsyth (golf), Lee McConnell (athletics) or Scott Harrison (boxing) will have youngsters rushing to the parks, tracks, gyms or driving ranges to try and copy them, Scottish sport would appear to be in dire need of a tonic, despite the well intentioned and generally well-received work of the Scottish Institute of Sport.

Few in football would argue against the notion that the current national team boss, Berti Vogts, is working with a squad of players many of whom would never have received an international cap in the eras of Mackay, McNeill, Greig, Law, Baxter, Johnstone, Dalglish, Hay, Law, Hansen, McLeish, Miller, McAvennie and Johnston. In rugby, against the odds, we can still produce many fine players but how much better equipped would we have been to claim a place amongst the world's elite if we could have invented a time machine to recall Andy Irvine, the Hastings brothers, John Rutherford, Gordon Brown, Finlay Calder and John Jeffreys. There are also many hundreds of dedicated swimmers in Scotland, yet Alison Sheppard's 2002 Commonwealth Gold medal in the 50 metres freestyle was this nation's first gold at any significant event since David Wilkie's Olympic victory in 1974. Similarly, 400-metres runner Lee McConnell is probably the only recognisable name in Scottish athletics, though it is usually her undoubted sex appeal which gets her a mention in the football-dominated tabloids, ahead of her still evolving talent.

When it comes to golf – a game we probably invented – our success with players such as Torrance, Lyle, Montgomerie, Lawrie and Forsyth in recent years has been more down to natural talent than any South African or Australian-style academies of excellence. The Scottish Golf Union did make an attempt to help the game's best talents in 1999 when it opened the Scottish National Golf Centre at Drumoig near St Andrews, but the lack of a proper business plan and a general lack of appeal to golfers elsewhere in the country led to the centre going into receivership in September 2003. However, if we measure a sport's success by popularity alone, no one would dare suggest that there is any malaise afflicting golf.

Horse-racing continues to attract huge coverage in the national press and remains a popular spectator sport. Hamilton and Musselburgh racecourses have made great strides in the past five years to leave Ayr, supposedly our premier track, trailing behind. Perth and Kelso have also moved with the times and it's to be hoped that the proposals to upgrade Ayr by the track's new owners do go ahead. In training terms, Carrutherstown-based Len Lungo continues to lead the way over the jumps while Ian Semple (Carluke) and Jim Goldie (Uplawmoor) currently have more firepower on the flat than Linda Perratt, the current occupant of Cree Lodge in Ayr, traditionally the most important Scottish yard. As many trainers have found in the past, however, it just takes one major backer to come along to turn things around.

Whichever way you want to look at sport in Scotland in these early years of the twenty-first century, association football is the national obsession and dominates every other team and individual athletic pursuit. Other team games like rugby union and cricket are, sadly for those who pursue them or try to promote them, minority sports. The most recent example of this was the publicity surrounding the 2003 Rugby World Cup in Australia. The majority of the Scotland players returned to a sporting environment in their home country where fewer than 8,000 out of a population of five million actually play the game. That is thirty-three per cent down on the official estimate of 12,000 active participants from the then Scottish Sports Council just ten years ago.

Scotland's world ranking in rugby union tends to hover between eight and ten. A similar mark in soccer would have the national team nominated as perhaps the greatest side ever to don the blue jerseys, but in rugby union it puts us about two notches higher than the sport's minnows. As the southern hemisphere giants, New Zealand, South Africa and Australia (a country which can boast 10,000 junior rugby players in Sydney alone) march ever onwards and upwards, taking England, France and Ireland with them, the three Scottish professional teams which supply the nucleus of the national squad struggle to excel in the Celtic League in front of a core audience of about 10,000 people.

On the club scene, the traditional breeding ground of future internationals but now searching to find a new reason for being in the wake of professionalism, a few hundred at best will escape from the supermarket trolley to go along on a Saturday afternoon. Even on Cup Finals day at Murrayfield, television producers have to position cameras so as not to emphasise the fact that there are 40,000 to 50,000 empty seats.

Rugby union, like many other sports, supposedly suffers from the nation's fascination with football. But why? Apart from home matches for Celtic and Rangers, no club in our supposedly "Premier" League regularly attracts more than 12,000 people to its home matches. Outside the top twelve, the fan bases are even more precarious, three and a half thousand being a big crowd in the First Division and, Greenock Morton apart, anything between 500 and 1,000 being the norm in the Second and Third Divisions. Other matches attract fans as well, of course, with a dozen junior clubs disappointed if they don't have 500-1,000 paying customers on a Saturday afternoon. Total them all up, however, and the football-going public in Scotland is only 275,000 people, about a twentieth of the population.

Interest in televised games is much larger: live Champions' League matches involving the Old Firm on terrestrial television attract one in three of the total viewing audience. Yes, we're certainly interested in watching the game from our armchairs – but are we producing the talent to retain that interest in the future? In probably the biggest match in its recent European history – against Manchester United at Ibrox in October 2003 – Glasgow Rangers fielded a team without a solitary Scot.

Even the so-called provincial clubs are now tending to field sides packed with Spaniards, Argentinians, Danes, Dutch and Finns. Encouragingly, there has been a recent trend by Hearts, Hibernian, Aberdeen and Motherwell to give Scottish youth a chance, but the message appears to remain that top clubs will go for the finished article for short-term success, rather than spend years and money rearing their own home-grown stars. That attitude has to change.

To take a snapshot of the game in 2003 is to see clubs bankrupting themselves trying to compete with the two main teams, Rangers and Celtic, who themselves are losing millions trying to compete with each other. It's a vicious circle and no one, it seems, can negotiate a way out. Football clubs simply seem to blunder on and on in the hope that someone will appear from nowhere on a white charger and lead them to financial security. Banks are unwilling to upset account-holding supporters by closing their favourite football club, despite the fact that if it were any other business, the windows would have been flush-panelled and the wrought-iron gates melted down years ago. In recent years, Clydebank and Airdrieonians have both gone to the wall with Motherwell falling into receivership and several others clinging to their existence by the thickness of their shirts. By a bizarre twist of fate, Airdrieonians were expelled from the Scottish Football League, only for some of their supporters to club together and buy the rump of the old Clydebank, reforming and calling themselves Airdrie United. Even more oddly, the new club parachuted straight into Clydebank's place in the Second Division after the old Airdrie had been expelled from the league altogether.

In the top division, the two Dundee clubs are contemplating a ground-sharing scheme to cut running costs while the two Edinburgh sides have discarded that same idea after opposition from both sets of supporters. Like Motherwell, which has been forced to act simply to survive, Partick Thistle, Aberdeen, Livingston, Hibernian and Hearts have been forced to slash wage bills to maintain the banks' goodwill. While not quite in the same class of penury, the days when Rangers and Celtic could offer foreign stars like Ronald de Boer and Henryk Larsson upwards of £2 million a year will be looked at with incredulity in ten years' time.

The reality, if sometimes flatly denied, is that both the Old Firm clubs would like to leave the Scottish game and play their football in the English Premiership. Rangers may have cooled slightly on the notion, but if Celtic's majority shareholder, Dermot Desmond, managed to find a way to escape the shackles of the Scottish Premier League, Rangers would undoubtedly follow. Both clubs need each other to survive and the thought of even a season going by without an Old Firm derby would be unthinkable. Likewise, the thought of one club fighting for a top six finish with the Manchester Uniteds, Chelseas, Arsenals and Liverpools of this world while the other battles for a play-off spot with Sunderland, West Ham and Ipswich, is one that neither could contemplate. For that reason, immediate election to the Premiership would be the preferred, if currently impossible, route to take, as the notion that both could be guaranteed to work their way out of the English Division One at the first attempt is a fanciful one. At the moment, any such move seems as far away as ever: the thought seems to be that if the Premiership or the SFA or UEFA are persuaded to move from their current position of blocking any proposed move south, it's feared the floodgates would open and Dutch clubs would move to Germany or Belgian clubs to France. With international league boundaries breached, national associations would lose control and national teams might be lost in the shifting sands.

Another problem: given the undoubted quality of at least two thirds of the teams in the Premiership every season, should both Old Firm teams be in England and one of them then suffers a recession of the type that Rangers endured in the early 1980s, or the one which Celtic struggled through in the early 1990s, the result would be footballing disaster. Imagine the scenario if either was relegated and then spent years trying to get back up. The calls for a return to Scotland would be resounding – but clubs left in the Scottish leagues would be within their rights to refuse them entry, or at best offer them a starting point in Division Three South, as it will surely have become by then.

Yet Scotland minus the Old Firm needn't necessarily be a black hole. Some argue that fans would flock back to the game in Scotland if their teams started the season with a chance of becoming champions and reaching the Champions' League. At present, the bookmakers tend to bet 200/1 bar two in their ante-post markets for the Scottish Premier League each season. Without the Old Firm, it is argued, Hearts, Hibernian and the two Dundee clubs would probably have a realistic prospect of becoming champions, with others like Dunfermline, Aberdeen and Kilmarnock regularly qualifying for the UEFA Cup too. The chances of more young players coming through the ranks at the top Scottish clubs would probably increase, particularly as foreign stars would be less inclined to seek employment here.

And the bigger picture?

Modern living will continue to exert a major influence on how much exercise people take, how much they participate in organised sport, and how much time and money they devote to being spectators at sporting events. Natural sporting ability will always come through, but raw talent still has to be coached. I wrote earlier that sport in Scotland could do with a general tonic, but the occasional boosts provided by Celtic's UEFA Cup run, Scott Harrison's world title success and the increasingly prominent performances by Lee McConnell on the world stage of athletics are all helpful.

The simple fact remains that we're not going to be able to turn the clock back to an age before satellite television and computer games, when children's main interests were outdoors and physical. Every other developed nation has to cope with the same problems. For a small country we're doing OK, but we still want to do better. Isn't that what sport is all about?

Concluding essay

The Gaels

Angus Peter Campbell

Dear Ken

Thank you for your very kind invitation to write a fee-less essay which as a poet I am delighted to accept as the norm. I remember once reading that when Tommy Docherty was manager of Manchester United and they got thrashed 6-0 by someone (I know that's hard to believe nowadays) he was being interviewed and in response to the first question, "How do you feel about today's result?", Mr Docherty famously responded – "Well, we got beaten 6-0, and we were lucky to score nothing."

So, for nothing – except that I like you personally, that I believe the institute's work is one of the few beacons of hope in our modern Scotland, and because you claim to have established the world-famous library on Raasay – here is my contribution.

I note that you have asked for essays on many different subjects, including Gaelic, but because Gaelic includes all these different areas in its world I will endeavour to summarise its historic and contemporaneous position in most of these fields.

Society

The last place where society has survived is in Gaelic-speaking Scotland. Even the grand-demoness Thatcher, as she announced the death of society, would have been invited in for a cup of tea and a scone if she'd come to a door in Barra. As the world falls and falls into and beyond and between its twin towers, the twin towers of tea and scones survive the grace-less holocaust. Thank God.

Politics

Gaelic politics – like all politics – consists of the struggle between the fact that Donald Archie (even though he lives in Peebles) inherited his late uncle's croft, while the one who could really do with it, and who could really use it – his late cousin's daughter, Dolina Mary – was overlooked. So she lives in her council house at Lochboisdale purchasing the tinned food from the Co-op while the land itself goes fallow under sheep and more sheep. Meantime, her two sons, John James and James John, are in the 5th Battalion of the Queen's Own Highlanders, guarding the peace or is it the war? – in Basra.

Education

I quote Iain Crichton Smith's Murdo: "When Murdo went to school at the age of four, he being then about three feet high, a starved-looking very tall thin woman loomed up in front of him. 'You will have to speak English from now on,' she said. Murdo did not know what to say as he did not know English." Nowadays, this entire process is reversed, of course. Increasingly non-Gaelic speaking parents are moving into the Gàidhealtachd and sending their children to Gaelic-medium schools, so that, now in 2003, this is what happens: "When Daniel went to school at the age of four, he being then about three feet high, a large very tall well-built woman loomed up in front of him. 'You will have to speak Gaelic from now on,' she said. Daniel did not know what to say as he did not know Gaelic."

Business and Economics

Business is the new disease that replaced cholera and tuberculosis, which tragically killed so many thousands up almost until the time of my own birth in South Uist in the 1950s. Since then, business has finished the process. In international terms (let's remember that Gaelic is international, and not just confined to South Uist) big business has destroyed the small, the good, the indigenous. That capitalist businessmen's club known as the EU is like Hydra: speaking with many liberal mouths the one message of profit. In the local Gaelic world, the disease of business is such that no progress can seem to be made without going to the LEC or the HIE or CNAG or Bòrd na Gàidhlig or the CCG or a 1,001 other acronyms loaded with a business plan which outlines all the right outcomes. In the Gaelic business world (as in every other business world) an idea which is vibrant, radical, rooted and visionary is dismissed as insufficient until it is made bland, manageable, definable and profitable. Until, in other words, it is killed. What purpose, after all, has a rainbow? Or a human being, come to that? It's a miraculous business that we have six children, without having had to go to a meeting for approval.

When I was young, there lived in a thatched house by the roadside between the villages of Garrynamonie and Smerclate two bachelor brothers, Iain and Alasdair Fhionnlaigh, and their spinster sister, Anna Fhionnlaigh. Alasdair, I remember, was very slow of speech, but when someone mockingly asked him one day (in Gaelic) how on earth he managed to survive he said, carefully and slowly, "Chan eil Alasdair a' cuir a-mach, ach na tha Alasdair a toirt a-steach" – "Alasdair only puts out what Alasdair takes in". Which seems to me to be the heart of what they call economics – and not just money economics, but environmental, linguistic, cultural and all other kinds of economics. For how indeed can we put out more Gaelic (or art or theology or care or love) than we take in?

Law

The notion of Gaelic – which I associate with grace and love and honour and dignity and culture – having anything to do with the law is as far-fetched as finding WMDs in Iraq. I will only quote St Paul: "Therefore, there is now no condemnation for those who are in Christ Jesus, because through Christ Jesus the law of the Spirit of life set me free from the law of sin and death." This Christmas time, my dear friend – this New Year – are you following the law that sets you free or the law that diminishes and brings not life, but death?

Religion

This is where we really excel. There is, of course, only one road to heaven – through Jesus Christ, and Christ alone – but that road is variously, and complicatedly, sign-posted within Gaelic. From the narrow single-track road of Free Presbyterianism to the high road of Catholicism, we have it all. If only we all got together, we would fill one church, as opposed to a scattering of pews in half-a-dozen buildings, often in the one village. Mind you I like the choice, which is one of the great liberating aspects of Gaelic Scotland, from the psalms to the quiet Sabbath that still (just) survives in a tragic, fallen world almost entirely given over to shopping-centre worship, seven days a week.

Medicine

When I have a sore leg, unfortunately I have a sore leg in Gaelic "tha cas ghoirt agam". However, I get diagnosed and treated through the medium of English. From a very young age this taught me that I was sick in Gaelic and healed in English, so of course for a very long time I daily embalmed my soul and spirit and mind and body in English because I wanted to be well and healthy like the rest of human-kind. Then one day I met Kenneth Roy, who had a sore leg, in English – or at least in Bonybrigg Scots – and realised that human weakness gave credit to race, language, colour or creed. Ever since I have spoken Gaelic, even to Kenneth Roy, and am now well. Oh, and I haven't even had time to tell you about the great Gaelic physicians, the Beatons, upon whom the best sound practices in Scottish medicines are based. Did you know, for instance, that according to an old Gaelic remedy a cold blister can be cured by rubbing a slug (a seilcheag) on it? Or that this is the perfect cure for earache – you put a limpet on the fire and remove when the juice bubbles, and then – when it is able to be borne – you pour that juice in the ear and stop the ear with a bit of wool that still contains the natural oil? Or that for stomach ache – if the patient is in desperation – you put a rope around his feet and hang him by the heels from the rafters? And then you repeat that at what is called "reasonable intervals". Thought not.

Also, did you know that if you sprain your leg – or indeed any part of your body – you ought to skin an eel in long strips and wrap it round the sprain as a bandage with the fat side in. The eel fat, you see, soothes and the skin, being elastic, will not bind too tightly. You then put the strain in a running stream (which might be difficult to find, granted, in our increasingly urbanised and environmentally-damaged universe). Really, the more I think about it, the more we ought to agree with New Labour and utterly abolish the notion of the NHS, and establish foundation hospitals throughout the UK, based on these very old practices. It would – trust me – save an awful lot of money. How about this cure for warts, for instance: put nine nines of the joints of the corn or oats in a secret place, such as under a stone. Do not go near them again, and as they wear away the warts will also disappear. Well, that would put paid to Proctor and Gamble as well as reduce our taxes, what?

The media

Broadcasting In the old days, every Highland parent had two ambitions for their children: that the girls would become teachers and that the boys would become ministers (or priests). Nowadays, they have all – like me – become television producers. Soon, there will be no fishermen, only presenters. No bus drivers, or nurses, or roadmen, or ministers or teachers come to that, but only journalists working for *Eòrpa*, discovering Poland and Serbia and Italy, much as their great-grandparents discovered them marching through muddy Europe in search of Napoleon or the Kaiser or Hitler. As Iain Crichton Smith, in the guise of his alter-ego Murdo once wrote: "The oral tradition? I remember that we used to sit around the fire in the cèilidh house reading *The Guns of Navarone* aloud. It took three weeks. Before that we had *Where Eagles Dare*. I read the *People's Journal*. The other day I saw a funny thing in it. 'Highlander in kilt wishes to meet another Highlander in kilt.' I listen to Scottish dance music as I am immune to it now, and it doesn't affect me. I had seven children. Most of them worked for the Gaelic BBC. Did you ever hear the programme *From the Slabhraidh*? It was my daughter Sheila that did that. It used to be on at four in the morning."

Journalism In the nation that has given us the *Sunday Post* and a national media owned by self-regulating capitalist conglomerates it is a miracle that Gaelic gets an inch of space anywhere. One of the invidious poisons at the heart of the Scottish media establishment is its so-called free press, which is essentially a national licence to print any old half-truths masquerading as journalism. The owners and the editorial teams – who are answerable only to the owners, such as the Barclay Brothers who own the *Scotsman* from some offshore island, and to the sales-figures and advertisers – set an ideological agenda which is narrow, self-fulfilling and life-denying. Oh for a press that would be expansive, illuminatory, literary, visionary and challenging. The *West Highland Free Press*, at its best, was that, but the only thing that I read nowadays that is expansive, illuminating, poetic, visionary and challenging is the Bible. But I'll say this – when Oor Wullie goes to Gaelic-medium, progress will have been made.

The Environment

This means that the thick-walled stone-houses, with their indigenous thatched roofs, were all knocked down to make way for ugly Department of Agriculture subsidised houses in the 1950s. Instead of local stone, concrete blocks. Instead of thatch, imported tiles. Instead of being one with the environment, it was like transporting Cumbernauld to South Uist. Well, have you seen these thousands of Army houses left in Balivanich? Meantime, the historic Ormiclate Castle in South Uist continues to fall to the ground.

Culture

Literature Niall MacMhuirich; Iain Lom MacDhòmhnaill; Iain MacCodrum; Ruairidh MacMhuirich; Murchadh Mòr mac Mhic

Mhurchaidh; Gille Caluim Garbh Mac Ghille Chaluim; Uilleam Ros; Eachann Bacach Mac Gille-Eathain; Sìleas Nighean Mhic Raghnaill; Gun Urra; Eòghan MacLachlainn; Donnchadh Bàn Mac an t-Saoir; Mairearad Nighean Lachlainn; Iain Dubh mac Iain mhic Ailean; Màiri Nighean Alasdair Ruaidh; Bean Ghriogair Ruaidh MhicGhriogair; Iain Ruadh Stiùbhart; Alasdair mac Mhaighstir Alasdair; Maighstir Ailein' Dòmhnall Mac Fhionnlaigh nan Dàn; Rob Donn. Or, as Sorley MacLean put it: "I am convinced that Scottish Gaelic song-poetry is the chief artistic glory of the Scots, and of all people of Celtic speech, and one of the greatest artistic glories of all Europe."

Film This means that we sit watching all that trash which everyone else sits watching on their digital channels. As in Livingston, so in Lochboisdale, as we sit and watch *Terminator 2* or *The Incredible Hulk*, or whatever other ill the other Republican leader (Arnold, not George Dubya) has left us as an inheritance. As a consolation, each Christmas season we can always watch the box to see how others imagined we imagined ourselves, from *Brigadoon* to *Rockets Galore*, from *Whisky Galore* to *Local Hero*. In an essay I wrote in 1986, I concluded: "The fact remains that the Highlands and the Western Isles, like all other communities, will continue to be inadequately and inaccurately portrayed as long as the Highlands and Western Isles do not have any real access to broadcasting power within their own areas. As long as they remain the passive recipients of television and film rather than its active participants they will be treated as peripheral and insignificant and portrayed as others see fit." Unfortunately, I am now less hopeful than I was even seventeen years ago, because if the partial localisation of the Gaelic TV industry over the last ten years or so has taught us anything it is that we, as Gaels, are as perfectly able to produce drivel as the next superior culture. "Anything you can do, we can do worse" ought to be the new motto.

Art Our most famous visual artists were, of course, Columba and his band of merry men in Iona, who gave us the world-famous *Book of Kells* which – for some strange reason (och, let's blame the

Vikings) – sits permanently under glass in Dublin. Now there's a famous Gaelic saying attributed to Columba which reads "Far am bidh bò bidh bean, 's far am bidh bean, bidh buaireadh" which directly translates as "Where there is a cow, there will be a woman, and where there is a woman, there will be temptation and trouble". This explains not only the monogamous male-only monastic settlements of Celtic Scotland and the hermit-cells on remote islands, but also our great historic achievement in the visual arts. Woman-less, we invented the marvellous Celtic circles which circumambulate around themselves eternally in unfinished strokes: pleasing to the eye, but going nowhere. Nowadays, with the firm establishment of gender equality, Gaelic art has become but a poor shadow of what it once was. It mostly consists of sea-scapes assembled, conceptually, by non-Gaelic speaking artists who have escaped to live in North Uist. The only thing that baffles me nowadays is not equality but how so much art constructed by non-Gaelic speakers, whichever remote island they may happen to live on, can suddenly be branded as Gaelic art.

Theatre It's all been theatre. Especially that time when I was about seven, starving in South Uist. We used to get a Milanda loaf occasionally between the seven of us and it was a race to hide your individual slice in the most inventive place away from your thieving brothers and sisters. Under the mattress, between two shirts, between two Beanos, strapped up your trouser legs. And then later we read that Harold Macmillan, meantime, had been telling us that we'd never had it so good. Compared to the Clearances or trenches or the more recent POW camps, I suppose he was telling a kind of theatrical truth. It was only later that I realised that Macmillan's story – like Bush's story and Blair's story since – was just that: a story. No less and no more legitimate than my story, which has remained more or less unspoken. I now also realise that the great Gaelic stories were the ultimate theatre – tales told by the fireside in the theatre of the imagination, where neither poverty nor Harold Macmillan nor WMDs nor Blairbush ultimately reigned. They became mere shadows flickering on the shifting wall as the peat-fire died, or flared.

Poetry The great Australian poet Les Murray, who visited Skye last year in tribute to Sorley MacLean, has already said it: "Poor cultures can afford poetry, wealthy cultures can't." Which is why we were once a great poetic Gaelic culture. But now that we all have satellite dishes, we can't afford poetry any longer.

Sport Have you ever fished on the lochs of South Uist? Or gone walking in Skye? Or have you ever watched Kingussie score yet another goal – Ronald Ross, inevitably – as they rattle off yet another Camanachd Cup Final? Or seen the wrestling at the Askernish Games? Or gone wind-surfing off Tiree? Goodness – did you never attend a dance at the Old Gym in Balivanich? Then you haven't lived.

Gaelic

One of the biggest myths connected with Gaelic is that it is a peasant language confined to peasants living in rural idyll or squalor, according to your ideology. Gaelic was, of course, at one time the royal language of Court – the language of power and influence in Edinburgh, not just in Stornoway. The long political – i.e. educational, legal, cultural, linguistic – assault on Gaelic is well reflected in the demographic map of Scotland. If you look at Scotland in 1500, for example, around seventy per cent of it was Gaelic-speaking, from the Lothians to the Western Isles. Each century has seen a physical, as well as a metaphysical, retreat so that now, in 2003, just over one per cent of the Scottish population speak Gaelic. This is the point, however: around fifty per cent of these are urban-based, and with the learner-native balance rapidly increasing in the former's favour we are increasingly likely to see the largest number of Gaelic speakers in the cities and not in the lonely glens. In other words, when the time comes, and the last linguistic trumpet is called, the last native Gaelic speaker will as likely be found in a high-rise in Drumchapel as under a thatched roof in Drinishader.

Aon uair 's gum bidh a' chànan aig teas meadhan gach earrann air a bheil sinn a-mach an seo, bidh adhartas air tachairt. Chan e Na h-Ealain Ghàidhlig, gun Ghàidhlig aig an neach a chruthaich an ealain. Chan e Craoladh Gàidhlig, gun Ghàidhlig a bhi aig gach riochdaiche 's gach neach-camara 's fuaim, a bharrachd air dìreach am presenter. 'S tha dearbh rud fìrinneach mu gach earran eile: lagh, film, slàinte, spòrs.